445014

FLYING RADIO-CONTROLLED

Model Aircraft

FLYING RADIO-CONTROLLED
Model Aircraft

Colin Bedson

THE CROWOOD PRESS

First published in 2007 by
The Crowood Press Ltd
Ramsbury, Marlborough
Wiltshire SN8 2HR

www.crowood.com

British Library Cataloguing-in-Publication Data
A catalogue record for this book is available from the British Library.

ISBN   978 1 86126 915 7

Typeset by S R Nova Pvt Ltd., Bangalore, India

Printed and bound in Singapore by Craft Print International Ltd

CONTENTS

PREFACE AND ACKNOWLEDGEMENTS

As a very young schoolboy I spent many happy hours at our local common watching a group of guys from the nearby town hand-launching flimsy, oily, diesel-powered free-flight models over the heather and long grass. My friend and I were fascinated by these models, even though, more often than not, they ended up with some cosmetic damage from hard landings in gorse bushes and the like.

I lived in the country, so I had little opportunity to visit the outlets where such models could be purchased and there was no one locally who knew anything about them. As a consequence my childhood passed into youth without my ever having a chance to indulge in this fascinating hobby.

During my early thirties, married with a young family, I was delighted to encounter a group of enthusiasts entertaining the crowds at a country show with a variety of model aircraft. The amazing difference was that these models were not just going where the prevailing breezes took them; they were going where the fliers wanted them to go! I was intrigued by this new aspect of the hobby and, while my wife and children went off to explore the rest of the show, I spent the most of day watching the model aircraft in awe.

I was hooked. I had to have one of these flying machines and, of course, the control equipment that would direct it where I wanted it to go.

Thirty years on, I have tried most types of fixed-wing model flying, including gliders, both flat-field thermal soaring and slope soaring, Club 20 racers, pylon racers and scale competition flying. (Helicopters, on the other hand, have never appealed to me, and I have not been able to justify spending my hard-earned money on a flying machine with rotating wings.)

I became a keen member of my local model club, where I acted as Events and Competition Secretary for a number of successive years. I also qualified through the BMFA (British Model Flying Association) as an instructor and examiner and was responsible for training a fair number of new members over the years.

Generally, club instructors do a magnificent job and their patience is commendable, but my experience and my attitude toward student guidance have shown me that there is a need for a dedicated pilot training manual to help beginners progress (alongside the tuition and support of their instructor) with greater confidence. Obviously, there is no substitute for supervised training and flying practice, plus the 'hands-on' help and support of an instructor, but this manual aims to provide a valuable resource of detailed information to supplement this practical training.

Radio-control model flying is a wonderful sport. If this book helps novice fliers learn to become proficient, then my aim will have been accomplished.

ACKNOWLEDGEMENTS

Over the years it has been a genuine source of amazement, even frustration, that, as far as I am aware, no one has ever produced a simple, all-encompassing tuition manual for model-aircraft pilots. Organizations such as the BMFA in the UK and the AMA in the USA do provide tuition notes for beginners, and many club websites offer 'notes for beginners', but there seems to be no one volume that takes the complete novice from beginning to end of the process of learning how to fly a model aeroplane. What is needed is a complete approach that not only guides the student through the programme, but also points out the dangers and obstacles that will be encountered along the way.

From time to time I have read through the guidance notes supplied with trainer model kits and they are often not entirely suitable for the rookie pilot. The notes on flying almost always fail to mention the rules and regulations governing model flight, let alone insurance requirements. There is rarely, if ever, any suggestion of 'getting help' or a warning of the impending dangers of going it alone.

This book owes its existence to my attempts to rectify this situation. I wrote two e-books – one covering learning with electric models and the other dealing with models using IC or glow motors – which were published through my own website. The response was very positive and a good number of people bought them. I was greatly encouraged by the feedback and felt that maybe a printed version would reach many more potential model pilots.

I have to thank my partner Carol for her unselfish encouragement and enthusiasm over the project. The original e-books would probably never have been written without her suggestion and encouragement. I also obtained the help of fellow model fliers here in Spain and must mention Peter Greet and his friend Dave Morley for their help in producing some of the photographs. Further thanks go to Howard Murphy of Mayor Models, Santa Pola, Spain, again for help with providing products and assistance with photography. Lastly, I have to thank the late Paul Landel of Just Engines for his professional expertise and assistance with some of the technical content for the sections on glow engines.

I hope that you will enjoy reading and learning from this book as much as I have enjoyed writing it. If you get just one useful tip or hint that helps you avoid an unnecessary accident or expense, then my efforts will have been more than rewarded. This is an addictive and challenging hobby. Have fun with it and fly safe.

Colin Bedson

INTRODUCTION

Welcome to the world of radio-control model flight. What hooked you on this fascinating but frustrating hobby? It is, after all, a hobby in which, if you take the wrong approach, you will almost certainly end up a disillusioned and poorer individual.

You have probably seen model fliers enjoying themselves at the club field, persuading their models to perform all sorts of manoeuvres. You may have watched in awe as the miniature flying machines seem to defy all the rules of gravity. You have probably thought to yourself, 'I wish I could do what these guys can do.' Well, the good news is that, with determination and perseverance, you *can*!

You need to appreciate the fact that these wizards of model flight have probably been flying planes like these for several years. Once upon a time, they were standing, watching, just like you, impressed by the skills of other fliers. Flying these aircraft is not impossible for you, but it will take time, practice, patience and money. The actual amount of time, practice, patience and money will depend on your aptitude, and your willingness to listen and learn. You will also need to accept that it will cost you – this is not a cheap hobby (although it can be relatively inexpensive compared to some other activities).

If you want to learn to fly a powered, radio-control, fixed-wing model aircraft, and you are prepared to *take advice*, this book will help you succeed, with the minimum of pain and disappointment.

BASIC ADVICE

The advice given here relates to fixed-wing model aircraft powered by two-stroke fuel engines or electric motors. The basics, as far as power systems, radio and starting kit are concerned, are also relevant for helicopters.

There are a couple of basic fundamental factors that must be accepted and appreciated before you start:

1. Where you are going to fly your model safely and legally.
2. Protection by third-party indemnity insurance.

The best way to deal with these essentials is to approach and join your local model flying club. Such organizations will, in most instances, have negotiated flying rights with a local landowner, council, and so on, while some may even own their own flying field. Most established clubs will be affiliated to the national governing body that controls model flying in their particular country. As part of that affiliation they will offer inclusive membership insurance at a fraction of the cost of an individual trying to insure himself.

Not only does club membership carry these most useful benefits, a club will almost certainly offer a pilot training scheme for members. Many clubs today even provide a suitable club trainer and control set-up on which beginners may 'cut their teeth'.

ESSENTIAL CONSIDERATIONS

If this reality check has not dampened your initial enthusiasm, you can move on to further important considerations:

- Where are you going to learn to fly your model?
- Who is going to teach you?
- What model will you choose?
- How are you going to power it?
- What radio equipment will you choose to control it?

Where to Fly

Unless you happen to own a large tract of open land with short cropped grass or an ex-military airfield with an old runway, you will need to join a club or arrange to fly on someone else's land. Whatever you do, you will have to abide by the regulations that control model flying in your country. The civil aviation authority that controls aircraft movement within your home country's airspace will usually have a set of strict guidelines for the operation of airborne models.

If you intend to go it alone, then it is your responsibility to ensure that you do not contravene these regulations.

If you join your local model aircraft club, none of the above will concern you. The club will have taken all necessary precautions and responsibilities to ensure that its members adhere to all the regulations. All you have to do is abide by the club rules and enjoy your flying and the camaraderie of the other members.

As a general rule, model club members are a very mixed bunch of characters and you are sure to find a few to whom you can relate. You will share many enjoyable times with them and you will also benefit greatly from the experience and expertise that they will be happy to share with you.

The Instructor

It is not completely unknown for individuals to teach themselves to fly model aircraft, but they are much more likely to encounter miserable failure than any sort of success. Without the help and support of an experienced flyer, you are almost certain to destroy your pride and joy at the first attempt. Gravity is a very unforgiving adversary and, unless you are very lucky, you will lose your initial confrontations with it. Even if you have a commendable attitude and a determination not to be defeated, the encounters will empty your financial coffers quite rapidly. Repairs or replacement aircraft, engines and radio equipment can be a major drain on finances.

Why make life difficult for yourself when a reasonable outlay will give you a full year's club membership and the help of a qualified tutor at your disposal? Most clubs provide free tuition for novice members.

A proficient instructor can be the best aid to your success in this adventure. Most club instructors have been through a process of selection and special training to provide them with the skills they need to teach others: the BFMA (British Model Flying Association) has a testing procedure for instructors and most affiliated clubs comply with the requirements of this programme by using only instructors who have passed this examination. Talking to each of the appointed instructors will help you find one to whom you can relate. Bear in mind also that your instructor has to have your respect. This relationship is very much a two-way exercise and requires you to be receptive and prepared to obey instructions as required. If the club appoints an instructor with whom you feel uncomfortable, do not be afraid to explain this to the training officer and find one with whom you are happy. It is very important that you and your instructor have a strong measure of both trust and understanding.

Once you are happy with your instructor, take some time to sit down and have them explain the programme you will follow; they will probably do this anyway. This is important so that you know exactly what will be expected of you. It will also give you some idea of the time frames required to fulfil the various stages of the programme.

Choice of Model

There are mixed opinions as to the choice of first model. Some suggest a fully built-up model, starting with a box of wood, glues, accessories and a plan. The theory here is that the construction process will teach the builder a great deal about the way the model works and how it will fly. This knowledge will help the student understand the laws of physics that apply to flight, the way the model travels through the air, and the forces that work on the control surfaces.

The downside of this approach is the time it takes to get to the flying stage. A rookie builder can take quite a long time to finish a model. Inexperience can lead to building errors that could make the model unflyable or, at best, a real handful and difficult to trim for stable flight.

Most modern Almost Ready To Fly (ARTF) model kits come with a high level of pre-fabrication and are designed to have the owner airborne in a matter of hours rather than weeks. The designers have done all the hard work and the prototypes have been fully tested and checked for their suitability as training models. In the hands of a competent instructor, most of these models will fly straight from the building board and will be easy to trim for stable flight. In addition, the

Typical trainer-style model.

student will be learning quickly on a plane that is relatively easy to fly.

The choice of models is almost endless, with numerous ARTF kits on the market. The range kept in stock at your nearest model shop will almost certainly reflect the most popular models that are sold – that is to say, those models that find favour with both instructors and students alike.

Recent designs have greatly improved and the standards of construction and finish are very good. Most of the models available look something like real aeroplanes and, with care and attention, will reward the owner with a model of which they can be proud.

If you have joined your local club, take a look at the trainers being used and discuss their choice with both owners and instructors. Instructors' opinions are particularly relevant as they will have experience of flying many different types. They will recommend types they prefer and you can guarantee that, if they are happy with a particular model, they will be comfortable training you on it.

A model with a wing span of 1.4m (55in) to 1.8m (72in) will be suitable. Most kits feature models with a span of around 1.52m (60in). These are designed to fly on a 40 to 50 size glow motor or 400 to 600 size electric brushed motors and are ideal. Choose a high-wing type for stability. You can progress to shoulder-, mid- or low-wing types once you have become proficient on your trainer type.

There are also a number of practical considerations that must be taken into account:

- ease of repair
- availability of spare parts
- stability
- control set-up
- accessories and equipment

Ease of Repair

Your first – and maybe your second – model could well be damaged as you learn how to fly, so you should look for a trainer that has relatively few parts, which can be easily repaired if they are broken. Wood and foam pieces are easy to fix, while moulded plastic, fibreglass or epoxy resins are more difficult to repair. Cyanoacrylate (CA) glue (sometimes called 'superglue' or 'cyano') and epoxy are the most common adhesives used for gluing wood parts together. Aliphatic resin or special white glues available from your model shop are excellent for gluing foam pieces back together.

Availability of Spare Parts

Often it is easier to replace damaged parts than to repair them. Try to select a model that has replacement parts readily available via your model shop from the manufacturer. Some model kits have extra wings supplied in case one is damaged beyond repair.

Motors (both glow and electric), batteries, ESCs (Electronic Speed Controllers) and servos can get damaged or worn out, but it is simple to replace such parts as required. It will not be necessary to buy a new model if any of these are damaged.

Bear in mind that, should any of these components fail in flight, they could result in the need to replace the airframe!

Stability

Some trainers are easier to fly than others. Talk to your instructor and other owners, to find out how stable the various models are.

A good indicator of how stable and easily a model will fly is how much wing dihedral it has and how long the tail moment is. As a general rule, a model with a fair amount of dihedral angle (5 or more degrees), and a fairly long tail moment, will fly with more stability and smoothly for ease of control. For clarity, refer to the overhead and side aspect diagrams of a typical trainer model. (The 'moment' – nose moment or tail moment – refers to a distance on a model forward or aft of the balance point.)

Control Set-Up

Before you buy a model, check its control set-up. There are normally two set-up options available:

1. basic standard primary control set-up: rudder, motor and elevator control.
2. four-function control: rudder, motor, elevator and aileron control.

Although you can learn quite satisfactorily on the first of these set-ups, you will have to progress to the second configuration eventually. If you can afford the extra function initially, you may just as well master all four controls from the outset.

Accessories and Equipment

Check to see whether the model you like comes with all the equipment you will need to complete the airframe. In the long run, it is less expensive to get everything in one package. Your kit should include all the materials needed to assemble the model (with the possible exception of glues). It is sometimes worth paying a bit more for your model if it comes with everything included. Buying the extras separately can add considerably more to the overall cost.

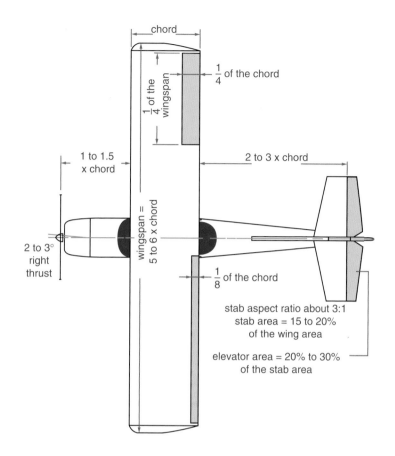

chord

$\frac{1}{4}$ of the chord

$\frac{1}{4}$ of the wingspan

1 to 1.5 x chord

2 to 3 x chord

wingspan = 5 to 6 x chord

2 to 3° right thrust

$\frac{1}{8}$ of the chord

stab aspect ratio about 3:1
stab area = 15 to 20% of the wing area

elevator area = 20% to 30% of the stab area

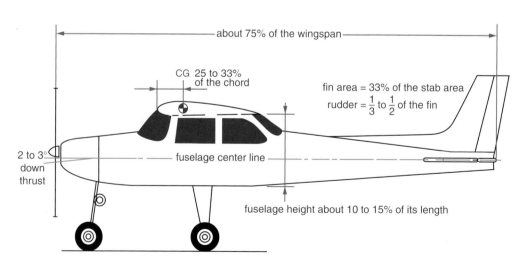

about 75% of the wingspan

CG 25 to 33% of the chord

fin area = 33% of the stab area

rudder = $\frac{1}{3}$ to $\frac{1}{2}$ of the fin

2 to 3° down thrust

fuselage center line

fuselage height about 10 to 15% of its length

Ideal trainer parameters and dimensions.

POWER PLANT

At this point you will have to decide on your preferred method of motive power: traditional glow power or the more modern electric approach.

Glow Power

Model glow engines have been around for many years and today a wide range of such engines are offered by numerous manufacturers. The technological improvements, modern materials and state-of-the-art precision engineering facilities used virtually guarantee that the current crop of products will give the user many hours of trouble-free flying. As always, though, this can only be the case where guidelines are followed and common sense prevails.

Another major benefit of choosing this type of power plant is that most instructors will have considerable experience of them.

Cost is another consideration. The type of sport glow engine that is suitable for a trainer model will be relatively inexpensive, will provide more than enough power for the model, and will be hard-wearing and durable. Glow fuel is relatively inexpensive and is normally readily available from model shops.

There are a couple of significant downsides to this method of propulsion: it is noisy, and the two-stroke fuel leaves oily residue on your model, equipment and hands.

Depending upon where you live, the noise of the glow engine may or may not be an issue. In highly populated areas, where open land is at a premium and flying sites that comply with the guidelines on noise sensitivity are becoming more and more difficult to locate, it may be a major consideration. On the other hand, if you live in an area with vast open spaces, it may be less important.

There are strict rulings on the flying of model aircraft with noisy motors in the vicinity of 'noise-sensitive buildings'. This is another good reason for joining a registered club. The flying site will have been selected to comply with these regulations and the club's rules on noise levels will reflect this requirement.

For many model fliers, the oil and smells, as well as the sounds, associated with model glow motors are precisely the reasons why they choose this type of power. They argue that much of the 'romance' of flying model aircraft is associated with the challenge of starting the motor, tuning it to its peak of performance, and then feeding the sounds, smells and the feeling of raw power into the sensory system. The throb, scream, roar (call it what you will) of the model as it soars overhead provides, for many, the major excitement of the hobby.

Electric Power

Over the last few years, electric power for models has become a truly viable option. The rapid development of new batteries with higher capacities and lower weight penalty, alongside the new generation of brushless motors, have made electric power an attractive option for the newcomer.

The power output of the brushless electric motor has developed to a point where it can now truly rival, and in some instances exceed, the performance of a glow motor – but at a price! As battery technology improves, so does duration. The latest generation of Lithium–Polymer (Li-Po, or Li-poly) batteries are capable of giving some models a flight duration of over 30 minutes – again, it comes at a price. Despite the developments, however, a recent comparison exercise undertaken and reported in one of the British model publications drew the conclusion that, with everything taken into account, glow power was still more cost-effective than electric power for systems with equal power output capability.

The major advantages of electric power are the absence of noise and the cleanliness. There will be no lost flying sites resulting from complaining neighbours and no spilled fuel or cleaning up your model at the end of a flying session.

No doubt the cost of electric power systems will gradually reduce with time and may well challenge fuel powered motors in due course. However, I ask you, did you ever see or hear a silent Spitfire, Hurricane or P-51?

Whichever mode you choose, be sure to follow the guidelines provided by the manufacturers and also take note of the advice given to you by your instructor and fellow club members, especially those who successfully employ your choice of power source.

CHOOSING AN ENGINE

Using Glow Power

The most suitable engine size for almost all trainers is 6.5cc. (0.40cu in or 'forty').

Two typical glow engines.

The choice of engine for a trainer is mind-boggling. With so many manufacturers, most of them offering several engines in the same capacity range, how do you choose?

You can buy cheap or you can buy reliable. A reliable engine starts, ticks over, runs and stops when it is meant to, and will probably cost £10 ($20, €15) to £15 ($30, €22) more than a cheap offering. If you enjoy the challenge of getting an engine to run properly when it does not want to, buy cheap. If you want to learn to fly, buy reliable.

A good engine does not have to be a powerful one. What you need in a suitable trainer engine is one that starts easily, is easy to set up and runs consistently. While you are still learning, most of the time you are unlikely to have the engine running at much more than half throttle. Ask around at the club and watch anyone else learning to fly. Notice how easy it is to get their engine started. Does the engine run consistently throughout the flight – full throttle on take off then back to about half throttle? Does it falter just after take-off or die in the air unexpectedly? As a fairly rough guide when you are observing others, a trainer should be airborne about five minutes after the decision to have a flight and should fly around for about ten minutes before landing. Starting difficulties, head-scratching, frustrations and bad language are indicators of possible poor engine performance and/or poor set-up.

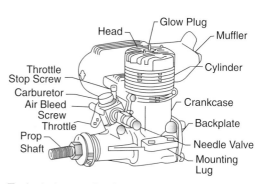

Typical glow-engine layout.

Talk to your instructor, who should be familiar with a wide range of engine types. Showing pupils how to start engines of all types is one part of their designated tuition programme. They will have learned to differentiate between those engines that start and run easily and those that can be generally tiresome. Select your engine carefully and look after it and you will be rewarded with hours of flying pleasure.

You will also need a set of accessories appropriate to your engine:

1. two propellers – one on the model and a spare, which for a 6.5cc. (0.40cu in) engine will probably be 10 × 6in.
2. two glow plugs – one fitted to the engine and a spare.
3. a spinner.

You may also want to consider a silicon exhaust deflector, which will help to keep your model clean by deflecting the exhaust away from the fuselage.

Using Electric Motors

As with glow motors, the choice of electric motor for your trainer is vast. There are many motors that are capable of delivering the power to weight ratio you require, but there are a number of options to consider.

Some kits are supplied with a motor/speed controller and battery specifically selected for the model. They are usually the cheaper versions and you will find that flight times will be fairly short because of the need to fly at full power throughout each flight.

For those kits not supplied with a motor, you can buy less expensive 'can-type' motors with brushes, which will perform adequately when paired with the correct electronic speed controller and battery combination. Again, the sometimes marginal power available will mean that full power is required most of the time.

Alternatively, you can invest in a more efficient brushless motor and combine it with the new generation of Li-Poly battery for higher power, lighter weight and more controllable flight – but at a price premium. The choice is yours!

Talk to your instructor or other members in your club who are familiar with a wide range of motor types. They will be able to advise

Brushed can 400 motor and brushless outrunner motor.

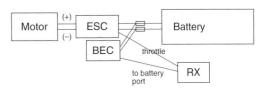

Electric motor power control (ESC/BEC usually combined for small motors).

you on the best combinations for your chosen model. Select your motor carefully and look after it and you will be rewarded with hours of flying pleasure.

You will also need a set of accessories appropriate to your motor:

1. two propellers – one on the model and a spare.
2. two battery packs – one to charge while the other is in the plane.
3. a suitable battery charger, appropriate to the type of batteries used.
4. a spinner.

Please remember to treat your motor (glow or electric) with the respect it deserves. Too much damage has been caused to various parts of the anatomy as a result of a flier failing to appreciate the awesome power of a model propeller spinning at a few thousand revs. These miniature power plants carry a

seriously damaging 'sting in the tail' if treated lightly. Also, you should not forget to fit a fuse between motor and speed controller when using a brushed motor (*see* Resources). You have been warned!

THE RADIO-CONTROL SYSTEM

There are many modern radio systems to choose from. Each manufacturer offers a wide range of options, from simple two-channel to computer-assisted eight-channel systems (and more!). The choice of system is limited partly by your financial budget, but also, as a beginner, by the advice you receive from your intended instructor. There are a number of good reasons why you should consult with the instructor, but the main one is that, if a buddy-box link is proposed (*see* page 19), your system must be compatible with his.

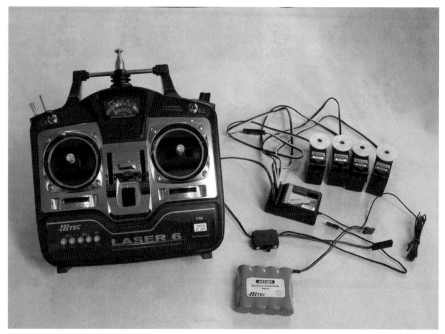

A typical radio-control system.

All standard radio systems consist of four basic components:

1. transmitter – the unit that takes the control input from the pilot through the gimbal-mounted sticks, encodes this input and sends it to the aircraft as a radio signal.
2. receiver – the unit that receives the signal from the transmitter, decodes it and routes it to the appropriate servo.
3. servos – these devices convert the decoded signals into a mechanical force that is directed via a linkage to the appropriate control surface.
4. batteries – the components that provide the electrical supply, enabling the other components to function.

Radio-Control Transmission Frequencies

The atmosphere surrounding the earth is filled with a myriad of radio signals providing information for thousands of different communication systems along with naturally occurring radio waves such as solar radiation. When you switch on your radio-control transmitter you merely add to this information blitz. It is therefore essential that the signals you transmit do not coincide with other transmitted signals; at the very least, they should be stronger than any other similar signal within the vicinity of your flying field, otherwise. your airborne receiver will have great difficulty deciding which signal to obey.

Specific frequencies are assigned for use with airborne radio-control (RC) models, and a beginner must ensure that the system chosen is tuned to one of these frequencies. Radio-control system manufacturers usually put a sticker on the outside of the carton that says 'For airborne use only'. There is a frequency reference chart available that lists the purposes of all the frequencies that are assigned for RC use. The radio system that is chosen must meet the 1991 specifications for narrow-band receivers, and it is the responsibility of the manufacturer to ensure that the equipment is certified to this standard. The owner's manual for the system will note that

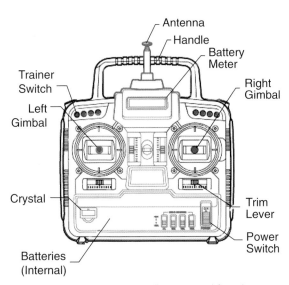

Typical transmitter layout – diagram and functions.

the requirements are met and many transmitters and receivers will have a gold sticker to signify this fact.

Radio-control systems may transmit and receive on either an amplitude modulated (AM) signal or a frequency modulated (FM) signal. Most modern aircraft control systems use FM frequencies as they are less prone to interference than the AM frequencies. Having said that, AM systems seldom have problems with interference. Most modern radio systems use an internal system, called PPM, to help to nullify interference.

Transmitter Control Modes

There are two primary modes of operation (meaning the way the gimbals are set up for operation):

1. Mode 1: most early radio-control fliers adopted this mode and it became the accepted configuration, particularly in the UK. Mode 1 has rudder and elevator on the left-hand gimbal (stick) and ailerons and throttle on the right-hand gimbal (stick).

2. Mode 2: in more recent times, many modellers have changed to the Mode 2 configuration, believing that it was easier to control the primary surfaces effectively with the same hand. Mode 2 grew in popularity and is used almost exclusively in the USA.

A beginner does not have to be too concerned about which mode to select since most manufacturers install the gimbals according to the most widely used mode for the country to which the radio system is being shipped.

However, it is important to consider the mode your instructor uses and the availability of your chosen mode from the supplier. All modern transmitters have the facility to change over the stick designations if necessary. Your user manual will provide instructions on how to do this.

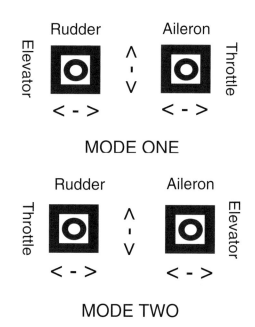

18

Buddy Box

Many instructors now use a buddy-box system, where there is a cable link between the student's transmitter and that of the instructor. This gives the instructor total control over the model in flight and the ability to transfer control to the student's transmitter at the flick of a switch.

In the event of the student experiencing a problem, this set-up enables the instructor to take control of the plane simply by releasing this switch. In essence, the student's transmitter becomes the slave to the instructor's master transmitter. The main advantage is the increased speed of transfer of control between student and instructor in the event of difficulty.

The Receiver

The receiver is a small rectangular sealed box, with a length of thin wire protruding from one end and a set of sockets and exposed pins at the other end. These sockets are provided to receive the plugs attached to the servos. Normally the sockets are marked with the appropriate designated function. The number of functions available will normally range from 4 up to 7 or 8, depending on the model purchased. There will also be another input socket designated for the battery lead.

There will also be a socket to take a receiver crystal, which will normally be fitted in situ when a new system is purchased. Crystals are usually supplied in matched pairs, designated Tx (Transmitter) and Rx (Receiver), and marked with the frequency value in MHz and/or the channel number. The Tx and the Rx crystals should never be interchanged.

Servos

The servo is the brute force of the system, converting an electronic signal from the receiver into mechanical output. Most modern servos have a central output shaft to which a variety of output arm types can be attached. If you purchase a new system the servos will usually arrive ready fitted, with a matching set of output arms. Alternatives will be provided, along with other accessories, in a plastic bag.

The direction of rotation of the output shaft can usually be reversed via a facility within the transmitter. Refer to your owner's manual should this be necessary.

THE BATTERY

Most modern outfits are supplied with a four-cell 4.8-volt 600ma/h Nicad rechargeable battery to power the airborne system. This battery must be treated with extreme caution and respect – ignore the manufacturer's guidelines as to its charging and discharging methods at your peril!

It is vital to understand that a battery failure during flight usually means major expense, as well as lost flight and training time whilst the resulting damage is repaired or replaced. This is equally important in respect of the transmitter batteries, which again are usually rechargeable.

CHAPTER 1
THE BASICS OF FLIGHT

Once you have gathered together all the essential components of your flight training kit and worked out what they all do, and recognized and accepted your responsibilities, it is time to look at how everything works, especially your model. A little understanding of the physics of flight will prove invaluable when things start to happen. Knowing why your model is moving in a particular way will help you appreciate the actions you need to take to retain complete control over its direction and attitude.

It is almost impossible to learn to fly without having the most basic of understanding of how and why aircraft stay in the air. If you are impatient to get going, you may be tempted to bypass this section, but you will eventually need to come back and read it. Fortunately, the rudimentary principles of flight are not too difficult to grasp and, once you are familiar with them, your understanding of what is happening to your model will become more clear.

FUNDAMENTAL PRINCIPLES

There are different and sometimes conflicting theories and arguments as to how airplanes fly, but the one accepted principle is that lift is generated as a result of the air pressure on the bottom of the wing being higher than the air pressure on the top of the wing.

Four primary forces act on an aircraft in flight: thrust, lift, drag and weight:

1. *thrust* is the force applied by the combination of motor and propeller pulling the aircraft forward.
2. *drag* is the resistance to forward motion of the aircraft by the pressure of the air against the forward-facing surfaces.

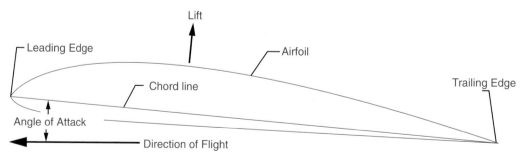

Lift diagram.

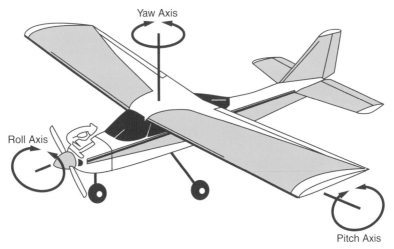

Axes of rotation.

3. *weight* is caused by the earth's gravitational forces acting on the mass of the aircraft.
4. *lift* increases as the velocity of the air passing over the wing increases or as the angle of attack increases as long as the flow of air over the wing remains smooth. Flight is achieved when the force of the lift equals the weight of the aircraft.

- In order for a constant speed to be maintained, thrust and drag must be equal.
- In order for a constant altitude to be maintained, lift and weight must be equal.
- In order for forward speed to increase, thrust must be greater than drag while lift remains equal to weight.
- To gain altitude, lift must become greater than weight.

An aircraft pivots about three axes:

1. the yaw, or vertical axis, which is controlled by the rudder.
2. the pitch, or lateral axis, which is controlled by the elevator.
3. the roll, or longitudinal axis, which is controlled by the ailerons.

The aircraft can pivot about any one of these individually or in any combination depending on the control surfaces that are moved and the direction of this movement.

Moving the rudder to the right causes the aircraft to rotate to the right about the yaw axis. Moving it to the left has the opposite effect and the plane rotates to the left of the yaw axis.

When the elevator is moved up, the aircraft will pitch its nose upwards, whereas moving the elevator down will raise the rear of the aircraft, and cause the nose to pitch down.

The ailerons move in opposite directions. When the left aileron is moved up and the right one down, the aircraft rotates to the left. Conversely, moving the left aileron down and the right one up causes the aircraft to rotate to the right.

At all times, the combination of these three control inputs determines the movement of the plane in relation to the surrounding air. Learning to fly your model depends on your ability to recognize these effects and to use them correctly.

CHAPTER 2
HOW THE CONTROLS WORK

Modern radio-control systems operate on a principle of 'proportional control'. This means that varying movement of the gimbal or stick will cause the control surface on the model to move in sympathy. If, for example, a control stick on the transmitter is moved half its full travel then the appropriate control surface on the model will also move half its maximum travel. Maximum movement of the stick will result in maximum movement of the same control surface.

The result is that the pilot has full 'proportional' control over the model at all times and can decide how gently or violently the model will react to the control inputs. During normal level flight the model is behaving in equilibrium, with all forces acting on it being equal. This is achieved by setting the throttle to a position where forward speed is constant and lift is equal to the weight of the model.

It is important to understand what effects the movement of the transmitter control sticks will have on the model.

Elevator Control

For the purpose of describing the control actions, Mode 2 (*see* page 18) has been assumed, as this is the most popular set-up for modern systems.

Pulling back towards yourself on the right stick will cause the elevator to move up. This has the effect of pushing the tail of the model down, increasing the angle of attack of the

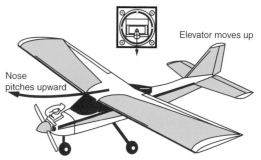

Nose pitches upward

Elevator moves up

Elevator control: right stick – pull back.

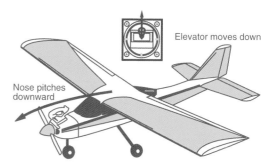

Nose pitches downward

Elevator moves down

Elevator control: right stick – push forward.

wing and causing the nose to pitch upwards. This also has the effect of increasing drag. To prevent the model stalling increased power is required. Stalling occurs when the air passing over the wing becomes turbulent and lift decreases until weight exceeds lift and the model begins to drop.

Pushing forwards on the right stick causes the elevator to move down. The tail lifts, reducing the angle of attack on the wing, thus reducing lift and drag so that the model nose pitches downwards. As the model descends, its speed increases until drag and thrust are again in balance.

Aileron Control

When the right stick is moved right the left aileron deflects down and the right aileron deflects up. This causes the aircraft to roll to the right. Lift is increased on the left wing, while on the right wing it is reduced. It will continue to roll as long as the stick is held in the same position. As the model rolls, the lift area of the wing effectively reduces, so the effective lift decreases. As the angle of the roll increases, effective lift continues to decrease and the model will begin to drop.

When the right stick is moved left, the opposite movements occur. The left aileron is deflected up and the right aileron down. Following the same reasoning as before, the model rolls to the left. The right wing lifts up and the left wing drops. The roll will continue for as long as the stick is held in the same position. Once again, as the angle of the roll increases, effective lift continues to decrease and the aircraft will start to drop.

Rudder Control

Moving the left stick in Mode 2 to the right causes the rudder to move right. This deflects the rear of the model to the left and causes the model to swing or yaw to the right, trying to rotate about its central axis. The left wing moves slightly faster through the air, increasing lift, while the right wing slows down, reducing lift. The combination of the yaw and the lift imbalance results in a gentle turn

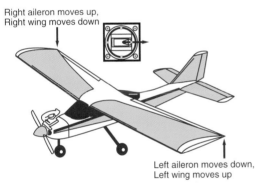
Right aileron moves up,
Right wing moves down

Left aileron moves down,
Left wing moves up

Aileron control: right stick – move right.

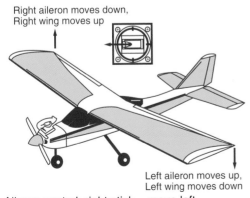
Right aileron moves down,
Right wing moves up

Left aileron moves up,
Left wing moves down

Aileron control: right stick – move left.

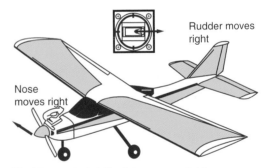
Rudder moves right

Nose moves right

Rudder control: left stick – move right.

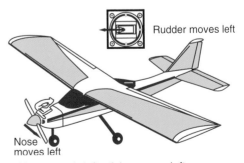
Rudder moves left

Nose moves left

Rudder control: left stick – move left.

23

to the right, as long as the stick is held in position.

Conversely, when the left stick is moved left, the rudder moves to the left. The rear of the model is pushed to the right, trying to rotate about its central axis. The right wing increases its forward speed through the air, causing an increase in lift, and this time the left wing loses speed and lift. The combination of the yaw and the lift increase on the right wing results in a gentle turn to the left, as long as the stick and rudder are held in position.

Engine Throttle or Motor Speed Control

The fourth stick function – forward and back on the left stick – controls the setting of the engine or motor rpm. When this left stick is moved forwards, the throttle of a glow motor is opened or the watts supplied to an electric motor increase, resulting in an increase in rpm and, consequently, in the speed of the model. Greater forward speed causes an increase in lift and results in a tendency for the aircraft to climb. Pulling back on the left stick closes the glow motor throttle down or reduces watts to the electric motor, resulting in decreased speed. Lift decreases and the model starts to descend.

It is important to appreciate that the effects of stick movement can adversely affect the flight of a model. These adverse effects are overcome by using a combination of control surfaces to achieve the desired positive results. When the right stick is moved to the left and at the same time pulled back, the resulting model response would be a banked turn without loss of altitude. The increased lift from raising the nose of the model compensates for the loss of lift in the left hand roll component.

Learning how to fly your model and to maintain total control of it at all times is the application of these principles. Mastering the combinations of stick inputs to position the model where you want it to be in the sky in relation to your position on the ground is the object of the exercise.

NB: the above advice is based on a four-function system, with aileron, elevator, rudder and motor controls. If you are starting out with a more basic three-function system of rudder, elevator and motor, you should substitute rudder whenever aileron control is mentioned. Most training models using three-function control compensate for the lack of roll control by having more dihedral. This causes the model not only to rotate about the yaw axis but also to rotate about the roll axis. Pushing the model sideways on to the air flow with the rudder changes the lift distribution in favour of the wing on the outside of the turn, causing the model to roll.

CHAPTER 3
MODEL PREPARATION

CONSTRUCTION

Construction of a trainer model is a very involved process, and too lengthy to be covered in depth here. Ensure that the trainer you choose has a good set of plans and step-by-step instructions that guide you through the complete assembly, including the installation of the radio system. A beginner with no experience in building or assembling flying models would be well advised to seek help from an experienced modeller to avoid mistakes that can have disastrous effects. This is another good reason to join your local club before you invest money in your chosen model and equipment. There is no substitute for experience when deciding what to buy and what not to buy.

Consider using a strong, slow-curing adhesive if you are building your model from a kit. This allows time to correct mistakes during construction. Aliphatic resins cure slowly but yield an exceptionally strong joint, and sand easily after curing. All joints that are subjected to high stresses, such as the firewall and centre wing joints, should be joined with a slow-cure epoxy.

Wing alignment is critical in the flight performance and stability of a trainer. The building manual provided with the kit should give detailed instructions as to how this may be accomplished and special care should be taken to follow these instructions.

INSTALLING A GLOW ENGINE

Most trainer-style models have an engine that is mounted upright, for ease of installation and operation. Usually it is not surrounded by close cowls and is therefore simple to access and to adjust.

Most kits suitable for the '40' size of engine come with nylon-filled engine mounts. These are easy to drill for the mounting bolt holes, both for the bulkhead position and for the engine lugs.

In some kits, screws are provided to fasten the mount to the bulkhead and/or to fix the engine to the mount. It is advisable to replace such fasteners with bolts and lock nuts to avoid loosening due to vibration. Nyloc nuts are highly recommended for this purpose and may be bought in the appropriate sizes from most engineers' supplies outlets.

Ensure that the linkage between the throttle adjustment horn on the engine and the servo inside the fuselage is as straight and as friction-free as possible. It is also recommended to use a nylon clevis to connect the linkage to the horn. This eliminates any risk of metal-to-metal vibration, which could potentially result in radio interference.

The fuel tank should be firmly positioned inside the fuselage behind the front bulkhead so that it cannot move. Wrapping it in foam will help prevent the fuel foaming through

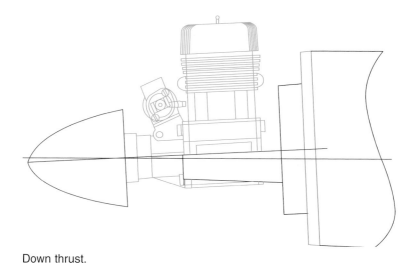

Down thrust.

vibration. Although the manufacturer will normally provide a measure of fuel-proofing for the engine compartment, it is well worthwhile coating the area with an epoxy resin to ensure the wood cannot be soaked with fuel and oil residue. This also helps to seal down the covering that overlaps into the engine bay.

Make sure all plumbing between the tank and engine fits correctly, and does not have any kinks or tight corners that are likely to restrict fuel flow. Examine your installation carefully for small nicks or pinholes in the fuel lines. Nothing is more frustrating than spending hours trying to get your engine running at the field, only to find there is a damaged fuel line allowing air to bleed into the fuel system. This also applies to the length of tube carrying the clunk to the bottom of the tank.

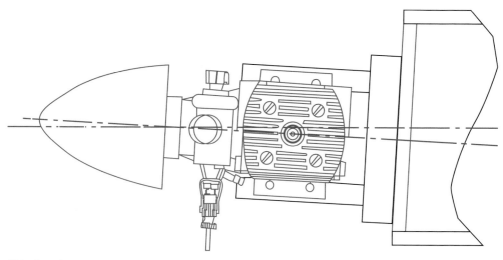

Side thrust.

Most trainer models will incorporate some down thrust and side thrust for the engine. This helps to overcome the effects of turn due to excessive engine torque or climb due to high lift coefficient of the wings. If you are in any doubt as to how this is achieved, consult your instructor or someone with experience who knows how to engineer it. Most modern ARTF kits have the appropriate offsets built into the fuselage, and all the builder has to do is mount the engine bearers and the engine. The necessary angles will be achieved automatically:

- to increase down thrust, add washers to the top of the engine mount
- to decrease down thrust, add washers to the bottom of the engine mount
- to increase right thrust, add washers to the left of the engine mount (when viewed from above)
- to decrease right thrust, add washers to the right of the engine mount (when viewed from above)

Fuel pipe connections should be as follows:

1. The fuel line from the clunk inside the tank should be connected to the engine's carburettor.
2. The overflow pipe should go to the top of the tank and be connected to the pressure nipple on the engine's exhaust.
3. A third line is often provided for re-fuelling. This should be plugged after re-fuelling to prevent air being drawn in during operation.

If you decide to fit a filter, this should be installed between the tank clunk outlet and the carburettor. This filter should be checked regularly for blockages to eliminate starting and running problems.

Make sure that the carburettor is securely fastened to the spigot on the engine and that the rubber seal ring is installed, to eliminate air bleed. With the throttle fully closed, check the air inlet on the carburettor fully closes. If it does not, adjust the throttle stop screw until it does. This will ensure the throttle servo does not stall when you close the throttle totally.

Check that the exhaust is securely attached and properly tightened to the engine cylinder using the gasket supplied with the silencer to minimize the escape of exhaust gases and oil from the exhaust manifold.

The propellor must be properly tightened. If possible, fit two nuts to the crankshaft or replace the supplied propellor nut with a suitable Nyloc version. In the event of a 'kick back' from the engine, the propellor may slacken, but it will not come flying off. Set the propellor in a suitable position for starting the engine. This is entirely dependent on who is going to start the engine and how. If you propose to use an electric starter (and this is strongly advised for a beginner), the position of the propellor is not critical. If you plan to to flick start the engine, get a 'chicken stick'. In this case the propellor should be between vertical and 'ten past the hour' when the engine is at 'top dead centre'.

If a spinner is fitted, the cut-outs in the spinner for the propellor blades should not make contact with the propellor blades. Check that the spinner does not come into contact with the cowling or fuselage front. This can be done by hand-turning the propellor and checking for adequate clearance behind the spinner (about 3mm or an eighth of an inch).

INSTALLING AN ELECTRIC MOTOR, SPEED CONTROL SYSTEM AND BATTERY PACK

The manufacturer's manual should give clear instructions for mounting your motor. The electronic speed controller (ESC) needs to be well away from the radio receiver and should be positioned where a good supply of cooling air can flow across it.

Setting up an ESC for the first time, with its many wires, can be disconcerting, but if you follow the instructions it need not be overwhelming. If you look at the top of an ESC for a brushed motor, you will notice five possible connections. On one side, there are two wires and on the other side is a red wire, a black wire and two wires leading to a servo plug connection. The two on their own (possibly blue and yellow or blue and white, or some other combination of colours) are for your motor. The lighter-coloured one of the two wires is your positive motor wire and the darker one is the negative. Just be sure to follow the ESC label markings for positive and negative.

Determining which wires go to which post of the motor can be tricky, because it all depends on whether the motor is directly connected to the prop or if you are using a gearbox. The rule of thumb for a direct-drive motor is for the shaft and prop to spin counter-clockwise when the shaft of the motor is pointed toward you. If the motor is connected to a gearbox, then the shaft should spin clockwise. If the ESC is connected to a direct-drive motor, the light-coloured wire is soldered to the positive side of the motor (sometimes marked with a red dot) and the darker wire is soldered to the negative side. The wiring is reversed if the motor is connected to a gearbox.

On the other side of the ESC is a red and black wire, which connects to your battery. Red is positive and black is negative. If you are soldering a connecter to these wires in order to mate the ESC to your battery pack, double-check the polarity of the plug before final soldering.

The servo plug is fitted into the throttle channel of the receiver. Read your RC equipment manual for the proper placement. The ESC should not be placed in the battery slot of the receiver because this will prevent you controlling it with the transmitter.

Most modern speed controllers, for the size of motor used in trainers, have a built-in battery eliminator circuit (BEC) that takes the motor battery voltage and drops it down to a usable voltage for the receiver and servos. Depending on the manufacturer, the voltage will range from 4.8 volts to 6 volts. This means you can eliminate the extra weight of the receiver battery.

The flight battery is the heaviest item in the power chain and needs to be well secured. It is disastrous to have a wayward battery pack smashing its way around the delicate equipment inside the model. Again, follow the instructions, or get help from an experienced electric modeller as to the best way to secure it. Fore and aft positional adjustment of this battery pack is often the chosen method of achieving the correct centre of gravity balance point for the model.

RADIO INSTALLATION

If you are a complete beginner, it is vital to get competent help with the installation of the control system in your model. At your local club, there will be a number of fliers who are willing – and, more importantly, able – to help you get this right. The brightest beginner is the one who visits the flying field and gets step-by-step advice during the building of their model. Your chosen instructor/test pilot will inspect everything anyway, but you will appear much more competent if there are only a couple of minor problems to be rectified.

Servos
Each servo must be mounted using the rubber grommets and eyelets supplied with the radio gear. They should be secured using the

four supplied screws. Tighten the screws just enough to ensure the servo cannot move under normal operational forces.

Many radio-control systems come supplied with a special nylon tray to accommodate the servos. This can make life easier if you mount the servos in the tray and then position the tray on suitable bearers in the fuselage using four servo screws.

Some models have servo cut-outs in a purpose-made plywood plate already fitted in the fuselage. Either way, check your servos are firmly held in place and cannot flex under load.

Servo arms must be retained, using the supplied self-tapping screws. Any unused output arms on the servos that might foul another moving part should be removed.

Each servo should be plugged into its appropriate socket in the receiver and pushed fully home. Any servo extension leads must be securely connected. A good method to ensure these connections cannot part during flight is to fold the extension and servo leads back alongside the connectors and wrap some electrical tape around the connection and leads.

The servo leads should not be in tension or stretched and should be neatly secured in the fuselage.

The Receiver

The receiver is one of the most delicate and sensitive components of the system, and must be well protected within the fuselage to prevent damage during flight. Check that the operating frequency of the crystal is the same as that of the transmitter and that it is fully inserted into the receiver crystal socket.

Pack the receiver in shock-absorbing foam and securely locate it in the fuselage so that it cannot move around or be damaged by loose objects or the battery in the event of a hard landing (also known as a 'crash'!).

Run the receiver aerial loosely away from the receiver to a suitable point for it to exit at the top of the fuselage. It needs to be held firmly at this point. The aerial should run all the way to the tail (without doubling back on itself) and must be secured. You can secure the aerial using a modelling pin pushed into the fin post and a rubber band attached to the aerial as a tensioner looped over the pin.

Battery Pack

The battery pack (not applicable if your electric motor system employs an ESC with BEC circuit) must be packed in shock-absorbing foam and securely located in the fuselage in a position where it cannot damage any other equipment. The battery can often prove a useful aid to obtaining the correct balance point of the aircraft. Apart from the engine, it is the heaviest component of the airborne system. It can usually be re-positioned to facilitate forward or aft balance adjustment, as long as it does not jeopardize other, more delicate equipment.

The battery pack to switch harness connectors must be firmly connected and secured as before. The battery pack and switch harness leads should not be in tension or stretched and should be secured tidily away in the fuselage.

Securely locate the switch and harness in a convenient and easily accessible location in or on the side of the fuselage. Many switch harnesses have an integral charging lead for the receiver battery pack. This charging lead usually comes out of the switch through the same hole as the lead that is connected to the battery. Make sure that this lead is easily accessible for re-charging your receiver battery ready for the next flying session.

CONTROL LINKAGES

The choice of linkage and delivery of mechanical motion to the control surfaces will depend to a great extent on what the kit manufacturers have provided. Whether they are snakes or pushrods, take particular care over measuring and cutting to length before you install them.

Clevises

Where threaded links are fitted (common with snake-in-tube-type pushrods and threaded piano-wire extensions for rigid pushrods), ensure that the clevises are screwed on sufficiently to allow the threaded portion to protrude through the clevis threaded portion. Ensure that the clevises for each servo are clipped into the correct control horn and are secured using the keepers provided, to stop accidental opening. Complete these connections for all four functions: throttle, ailerons, elevator and rudder.

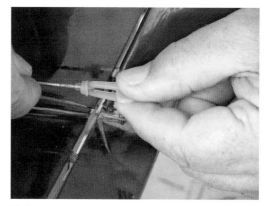

Fitting clevis to rudder horn.

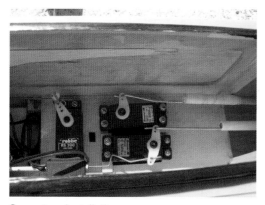

Servo tray installation.

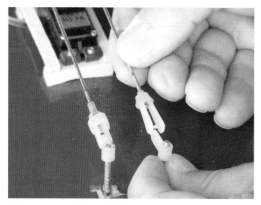

Aileron servo installation.

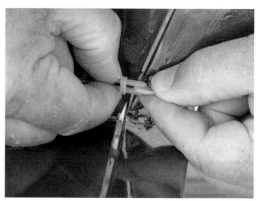

Push keeper over clevis.

Pull firmly on all threaded clevis/rod connections to ensure that the clevises cannot 'jump' threads when direct force is applied to them. At the small sizes of thread commonly used for these functions, US and metric threads can be interchanged. It is possible to screw a metric clevis on to a US thread but it will be a loose fit and could slip, with catastrophic results.

If screw clamp clevises are supplied, check that the screws are tightened fully and that the clamping mechanisms do not slide on the pushrods.

Pushrods

Snake-type pushrods are normally supplied with threaded wire inserts to which the clevis is attached. Ensure that this threaded insert is screwed at least 5mm $\left(\frac{3}{16}\text{in}\right)$ into the pushrod and that it cannot be pulled out. The snake outer of the pushrod must be securely fixed to a rigid structure so that it cannot flex during operation.

Rigid (balsa or spruce) conventional pushrods usually have metal rod attachments for the clevises that should be glued and bound to the pushrod. No movement is permissible where these components join.

Screw clamp fittings should be fitted so that only about 3mm $\left(\frac{1}{8}\text{in}\right)$ of the pushrod protrudes beyond the clamping mechanism. This ensures that they cannot foul any other controls, leads, and so on.

STATIC TRIMMING

'Static trimming' begins on the workbench. If you are building from a kit, you have total control over the model's final outcome. If the model is an ARTF, all of the components are already built and covered. As you assemble the model, there are steps you can take to ensure that it is properly aligned. The assembly instructions should provide guidelines for ensuring the stabilizer and fin are correctly set in the fuselage before gluing.

Wing Alignment

Most ARTFs are built wing first, and this establishes a good foundation from which to build. If your wing is in two panels that need to be joined, it is most important to make sure that they are aligned with each other; the trailing and leading edges should be even. If they are not, the wing will appear to be warped or twisted, and that will cause the model to roll in flight. If your wing is one-piece, sight down its trailing edge, and check for warps.

If you have access to an incidence meter, place it at various points along the wing. If the numbers do not match at each point then the wing is not straight. Finally, place the meter at each wingtip and take a reading. Again, if the numbers fail to match you will know that it is warped. To remove the warp, twist the wing in the direction opposite to the warp, and apply heat.

After you have attached the wing to the fuselage, you need to make three checks:

1. Is it centred from side to side?
2. Are the wingtips an equal distance from the centreline of the fuselage at the tailpost?
3. When viewed from the rear of the model, is the wing horizontal?

Check the centring by measuring from the side of the fuselage to the wingtips. Use the same reference point on both sides; the distance to each tip should be the same. If it is not, slightly enlarge the holes for the wing dowels in the fuselage and the bolt holes in the wing until you can centre the wing.

Next, take a length of string or thread that will not stretch under tension and tie it to a large T-pin. Insert the pin on the fuselage's centre-line at the rear and stretch it to a wingtip. Wrap a piece of masking tape around the string, and mark it where the thread meets the wingtip and trailing edge. Swing the string over to the opposite wingtip. With a bit of luck, the mark will line up on the corner. If it does not, mark it again and measure the distance. If it measures a quarter of an inch between the marks, for example, you will need to move the wing by half of that, or an eighth of an inch. If you have enlarged the dowel or the bolt holes, fill in any excess gaps with scrap wood so that the wing will be in the same position each time you mount it.

Now check that the wing is horizontal. With the wing installed in the fuselage, stand several feet behind it and see whether the fuselage leans to one side or the other. If it is crooked, sand the high side of the wing saddle to raise the low wingtip.

31

Balancing the Model

Before checking the centre of gravity (CoG), you need to balance the model laterally. To do this, make a cradle to support the model by its nose and tail, or have a friend hold one end while you hold the other end by the spinner or the prop. If your model is glow-powered, be sure to remove the glow plug from the engine so that its compression does not prevent the model from tilting. If one wing panel is heavier than the other, it will hang low. Add weight to the lighter wing panel to correct this. You can do this by pushing small nails into the wingtip until balance is achieved.

The model's CoG plays a big role in the way in which it flies. Initially, balance the model according to the manufacturer's recommendations. This represents a starting point for flight safety during the first few flights.

Finally, before heading to the flying field, seal all of the hinge gaps. Sealing the gaps not only makes the control surfaces more responsive but also makes control-surface flutter less likely. Use clear Magic Tape or matching covering material.

The easiest way is to unhook the pushrods from the control surfaces, fold them over towards the top of the flying surface as far as you can and then apply a strip of material along the underside of the hinge line. When the control surface is returned to neutral, the gap seal will hardly be visible.

CONTROLS FAMILIARIZATION

Now that your model is statically trimmed and ready for flight testing, it is a good idea for you to familiarize yourself with its control functions – which sticks do what to which controls. You may have read about the theory of flight control but there is no substitute for experiencing the nature of these functions.

Connect up the receiver battery and the transmitter to the charger and give them both a good overnight charge. Follow the instructions in your user manual.

Once the batteries have had a full initial charge, disconnect the charger and tuck the charging lead to the receiver battery well away from any control linkages. Connect the aileron servo lead to the correct input socket on the receiver and assemble the wing to the fuselage. The way you do this will depend on the manufacturer's chosen method of fixing (wing bolts or rubber bands).

Place the model on a level surface in front of you, with the nose pointing away from you, switch on the transmitter first, followed by the receiver switch; the order of switching on is most important. You may detect an initial jitter of the control surfaces before the servos centre and the control surfaces settle at their neutral positions. If they do not settle, you need to make adjustments to the appropriate clevises. All control surfaces should be exactly in alignment with the fixed part of the flying surfaces.

Assuming that you have done this and everything is as it should be, spend some time gently moving the transmitter sticks one at a time. (If your model is electric, *do not* operate the motor speed control function; leave this alone!) Observe the effect this movement has on the designated control surface and how the movement is totally proportional to the amount of movement you make with the stick.

As you make these control inputs, try to imagine the effect they would have on your model in flight. Refer back to the diagrams on pages 21–23 to help you become familiar with the concept.

Once you are happy that you understand these independent functions, try mixing two inputs at a time and again try to visualize the effect on the model in flight. For example, first move the aileron stick a little to the right and at the same time move the same stick back towards your body as you are holding the transmitter. The left aileron will drop, the right aileron will rise and the elevator will also rise. What can you deduce from these movements? Aileron movement causes the model to rotate around its roll axis. The combination of left aileron dropping and the right aileron rising gives more lift on the left side of the model and less lift on the right side, so the model rolls to the right.

At the same time the elevator rising causes the tail of the model to be pushed down and the nose rises, so the model has a tendency to rotate about the pitch axis. The combined effect of these two reactions is the model banking and turning to the right. This combination is the basis of every bank and turn manoeuvre you will make with your model.

Next, try every movable surface combination you can and try to work out for yourself the overall effect of these controls on the flight pattern. Do not worry too much about the throttle control at this stage; just remember that, generally speaking, the more power you apply, the more extreme the effective control movement. Work at developing a broad appreciation of the way your model is going to behave when you move your transmitter sticks.

When you are happy that you have a good understanding of the model's reactions to your control inputs, turn the plane around so that it is facing towards you and repeat the above exercises. This should give you an important appreciation of the reversal effect associated with the control surface movements, in particular the ailerons and rudder.

Once you have finished this exercise, switch off first the receiver then the transmitter. If you intend to visit your flying field the next day, do not forget to recharge both the transmitter and receiver batteries overnight.

Note: always switch your radio-control system on and off in the following sequence:

ON: transmitter first, receiver second;
OFF: receiver first, transmitter second.

CHAPTER 4
AT THE FLYING FIELD

At last the day will arrive when you will be ready to have your model checked out for its first flight. You will probably feel a combination of excitement, trepidation, impatience and pure fright! All of this is totally normal – after all, you will have invested quite a bit of hard-earned cash as well as serious hours in getting your model ready for this momentous day.

Test pilots of full-size aircraft always get nervous over the first flight of a new prototype, so you are in good company. Your instructor will probably be feeling just a little apprehension over the responsibility of getting this new model airborne – it is a journey into the unknown for both of you.

You should try not to worry too much. If you have done all your checks, and followed all the good advice you have been given, then everything should go according to plan. Your instructor will have experience of handling tricky situations and overcoming problems. The model will be examined with a fine-tooth comb before any attempt is made to fly. Any glaring errors will be noted and rectification must be carried out at the field, if possible, or back home in the workshop.

Each piece of equipment should be checked out by the instructor to ensure that it works properly. You can be assured that there will be no test flights if everything is not 100 per cent to the satisfaction of your instructor and/or the club safety officer. The model must be checked for correct balance then test flown and adjusted for safe flight. If the instructor feels that there is a serious problem with the aircraft, it must be corrected before you attempt your first flight. Only when all of the equipment and the model have been approved by your instructor should any training begin.

FIRST VISIT

Your first visit to the field will have nothing to do with flying the model. Before you reach the stage of actually taking the controls, you need to be made familiar with the site facilities and layout. You will be shown where to park, where to place your model in the pits, and, most importantly, how to use the frequency control system.

Make sure you understand the site layout, the transmitter control procedure and the flying area. Make sure you clearly understand the areas in which you may fly; if in doubt, ask.

The skill of flying radio-controlled models is not easily acquired, and as a beginner you need all the help you can get. Joining a club

First flights.

and enlisting the support of experienced model flyers is the quickest road to success – and the cheapest! Do remember, however, that your instructor is only human, and can make mistakes like anyone. He will teach you to the best of his ability and you should not blame him for any mishap that might occur during your tuition. Just like you, he is there to enjoy our hobby.

Following a few general tips will help make those first few attempts go as smoothly as possible and guide you towards getting a feel for the model in flight:

- Be gentle with the controls. It takes very little movement to get the model to execute a manoeuvre. Remember that the greater the stick movement, the more the control surface moves, and the more the model will respond.
- As long as the stick is held in a control position, the manoeuvre will continue. This is a most important consideration when using the ailerons. When the stick is moved to roll the model, it will continue to roll as long as the stick is held in that position.
- Fly in to a manoeuvre and then fly it out of it. It takes equal and opposite controls to overcome a manoeuvre and return to normal flight. A turn requires the movement of the ailerons in the desired direction of the turn. To recover from the turn, opposite aileron input is required.
- Always remember that when the model is flying towards you, the aileron control inputs appear to be reversed. When the model flies away from you, in order to correct a dropped wing you push the stick the opposite way; when the model flies towards you, a dropped wing is corrected by pushing the stick towards that dropped wing.
- Keep the model high – to quote a certified Flight Instructor: 'The two most useless things to a pilot are air above the model

and runway behind the model.' If you get into trouble you need plenty of air below the model to recover. When landing, the runway that is behind the aeroplane after touchdown is wasted because there is less runway from which to take off again in case of trouble.
- Keep the model in sight. Do not fly too high or too far away. Although your trainer model may seem fairly large, it is easy to get it far enough away so that it is difficult to see its orientation. Do not fly into the sun. A moment of blindness caused by the sun can be long enough to lose a model.
- Do not become discouraged. There will be times when nothing seems to go right and each manoeuvre results in a near-catastrophe. Everyone who flies radio-controlled models today has been through this situation; it is all part of the learning curve. Do not give up. The next session will be better.
- Do not panic. When a manoeuvre goes wrong, take all the time necessary to recover from the mistake. Panic will cause you to over-control your attempt to recover and cause the condition to worsen in the opposite direction. Although your instructor may seem to be a casual observer standing at your side, he will be watching in case you get the model into a dangerous situation.

The first few flights will begin with your instructor doing the take-off and checking out the model. You should watch the model as the instructor explains each control movement being used. This will give you an insight into what is required to execute a take-off. The same will be true for the landing. Learning to land a model correctly is by far the most difficult part of learning to fly. The model is most vulnerable when on the approach to landing because of its close proximity to the ground and its slow air speed. The reduced responsiveness to control input and the disorientation due to reversed control also represent a serious challenge.

When your instructor has flown the model and is happy that everything is satisfactory, the time will come for you to take the controls for the first time. The instructor will take the model to sufficient altitude, usually 150 to 200ft, and will ask if you are ready to take control.

It is normal to be nervous at this point!

If you are using a buddy box, when the instructor is happy that the model is totally stable and airworthy, he will give control to you by pressing and holding the trainer switch. You will be told the manoeuvres to perform and how each one is to be done. You will receive instructions as to how to improve each manoeuvre as it is being done.

The first manoeuvres will be gentle turns left and right, flying ovals around the field, and flying rectangles and figure of eights. Each manoeuvre serves a purpose in building your skill. You will progress to steeper turns, slow flight and stall recovery, each in itself a manoeuvre that is required if you are to master a landing.

If at any time you should get into difficulty, your instructor can take control of the model simply by releasing the training switch. In this way, a mishap can be avoided as the instructor takes the model back to a safe altitude. The instructor will not let a situation build to a point that is beyond his ability to recover, yet he will allow you time to attempt the recovery on your own.

The buddy-box system makes this close control much easier for both you and your instructor. It is not impossible to learn without this facility, but there will be a greater delay between your loss of model control and your instructor retrieving the transmitter in order to rectify the situation. Valuable seconds can be lost during the hand-over.

FINAL PREPARATIONS

Final Checks

When you are familiar with the flying site and its layout, and have a general idea about the procedures involved, you will be ready for the first test flights. Before the model is launched, however, your instructor will take great pains to check out every last detail of its integrity. He will want you to have the best possible chance of accomplishing as safe and event-free a first flight as possible.

A number of checks should be carried out:

1. Centre of Gravity (CoG): this should be checked 'dry', so ensure that the fuel tank is empty. The CoG should be within the limits specified by the model manufacturer. On a straight-wing trainer, this is about one-third of the way back from the leading edge of the wing.
2. Tracking: a successful take-off is greatly aided if the model runs freely in a straight line. Your instructor will place the model on the runway and gently push it forwards to see how it tracks over the ground. Any deviation from a straight line should be adjusted by screwing the nose leg clevis either in or out, depending on which way the model swings off track. Be sure to check the clevis is properly clipped into the control horn after adjustment and that the keeper is refitted correctly.
3. Frequency: your instructor will ensure that you have sole use of the frequency you will be using by obtaining the appropriate frequency peg. If you are uncertain of the reason for this control, discuss it with the instructor so that you fully understand the frequency control system in operation.
4. Radio (fouling): the transmitter must be switched on before the receiver (never the other way round). Move all the transmitter controls into all possible positions and combinations (except motor speed control

with an electric model, unless the model is properly tethered or held), remembering to move all of the trims as well. There should be no interference or binding of any of the controls. If the wing is fitted, the chances are that you will not be able to see what's going on inside the model, so listen closely! Any audible buzzing means you have a stalled servo(s).

5. Range (motor not running): with the transmitter aerial extended no more than 50mm (2in) (some transmitters put out virtually no signal with the aerial fully inside the transmitter), move at least 30m (90ft), or thirty paces, away from the model. You should have full control of all the flying surfaces at all times. This can be verified by moving the control sticks around. (Get your instructor to check all movements are correct and control is maintained.) There should be no occurrences of the control surfaces not moving when the sticks are moved. There should be no juddering of the control surfaces.

6. Failsafe: if you have a PCM radio fitted with a failsafe facility, follow the instructions in the manual to set the throttle control to reduce to stop or tick-over as a minimum precaution. Set the aileron stick to maximum right or left, elevator to maximum up or down, rudder to maximum right or left deflection, and throttle to idle. Switch off the transmitter only. All the controls should go to their pre-set conditions but, most importantly, the throttle must close to either 'tick-over' or 'stopped'. If you are satisfied that the controls are doing what you want of them, switch the transmitter back on. If not, repeat this process until you are.

Starting a Glow Motor

After all the final checks have been carried out, your model is to all intents and purposes ready for its maiden flight. It is now time to start the engine and set it up so that full control is possible during the flight. Ideally, you should run at least one tank of fuel through the engine on a rich setting to loosen up the parts, and ensure maximum lubrication whilst this is happening.

Some manufacturers supply their engines with the carburettor separate. If this is the case with yours, get the instructor to check you have fitted it correctly and that it is totally secure in its mounting spigot.

The fuel control needle will need to be set according to the manufacturer's recommended setting for the first start-up. Once running there will almost certainly be a requirement to re-adjust this setting for satisfactory running. Your instructor will demonstrate how to fuel, prime and start your engine safely and how to adjust it for optimum performance.

After these demonstrations, you should be able to carry out these procedures yourself. They are very straightforward, although starting the engine will take some practice. Remember that the instructor is always there to prompt or assist you.

Taxiing Trials

With the glow motor running smoothly at tick-over and slightly rich, or your electric motor stopped, your instructor will ask you to place the model on the runway. Before taking off it is important for the instructor to get a feel for how the model handles under power on the ground. Some models have a tendency to swerve either left or right and can be quite difficult to control during the take-off run.

It is also important to find out how the model will steer. The size of its turning circle will be relevant, as it may be necessary to bring the model back to the take-off point again. If you are flying from a concrete or tarmac runway, handling should be much easier and more accurate than from a grass strip. Grass has quite a drag effect on the model's wheels and can cause it to steer less accurately than on a smooth surface.

FIRST FLIGHT

When you have made all your final preparations, and your instructor has carried out those final checks, the moment will arrive when you will discover whether all the meticulous care and attention you have put into your pride and joy has been worth it. Although you will not be flying the model yourself, seeing it take to the air for the very first time can be one of the most exciting moments of the whole process of learning to fly.

Having eliminated any obvious problems, your instructor will be ready to fly the model. Just stand back and enjoy the sense of elation as your instructor puts the model through its paces. Do not worry if you see him making adjustments on the transmitter trims during this flight. Very few brand-new models will fly absolutely straight and level without some slight adjustments here and there.

After a few circuits, the instructor will probably be ready to bring the model in for its first landing. This can be one of the most critical moments for an untried model, as no one can know exactly how it is going to handle on its first landing approach. Having said that, unless they are dramatically out of trim or overweight, most trainers are relatively simple to land and the event should pass without incident.

Once the model is back in the pits area, motor stopped, receiver and transmitter switched off, you can stand back and congratulate yourself on a job well done. Do not forget to thank your instructor for his expert handling of your model. Now you know that it flies, there is nothing to stop you becoming a successful model-aircraft pilot.

This is the point at which your instructor will go through a 'postmortem' of the flight and will show you how to make any changes to the linkages that may be necessary to incorporate the trim changes made during the flight. This means that the next time the model takes to the air, all the trim levers (apart from the throttle trim) on your transmitter should be centralized, with the model flying 'hands off' in the straight and level attitude.

It should be possible to set your model flying straight and level into wind, let go of the transmitter sticks and, providing the wind conditions are reasonably light and smooth, expect it to fly exactly as it has been set.

Your instructor may want to give the model several test flights before he is ready to hand over the transmitter to you. Be patient! There are very good reasons for this approach. Your instructor will want to be absolutely certain that you have the best opportunity to control the model effectively once you take over. If he is struggling to control the model, then you it is more than likely that you will also struggle; that is the last thing you need when you are learning.

If this is the sum total of achievement during this first visit to the flying field, you will have had a successful day. The model is proven, your instructor is satisfied with its flight characteristics and you go home with your aeroplane intact. Your patience will be rewarded with the opportunity of your first hands on experience the next time out. Also you will have had an opportunity to discuss the model's handling traits with your instructor. If you take with you a note pad and pen you can write down any important points to remember.

TAKING THE CONTROLS YOURSELF

Whether your first hands-on experience occurs on the same day as your test flights or not, it will certainly be a memorable event for you. Although you are likely to have control for only a few minutes during this first flight, savour it; it is a special occasion and you will feel a sense of pride and elation. You will probably be very nervous, too, and may give your instructor a few moments of trepidation. Try not to panic – your instructor is right there at your side, ready to take over if you get yourself into a situation from which you cannot recover.

Try to remember that control inputs from the transmitter need not be excessive. Over-controlling will lead to problem situations, whereas gentle control movements will create wide, smoother manoeuvres that will give you time to think about your next control input. Your instructor will be talking to you all the time, giving you advice on how to get the model to fly in a controlled manner and to be where you want it to be.

Flying a model aeroplane is all about making it do what you want it to do, and not simply reacting to the model going where it wants to go and then trying to get it back under control.

Once the model is safely back on the ground after your first hands-on experience, it is time to take a deep breath, relax and enjoy the sense of achievement. Discuss the event with your instructor and try to learn from any errors you made during your time in control.

As with any acquired skill, the more practice you get, the quicker you will succeed and the more competent you will become.

SOME BASIC MANOEUVRES

Preparations
At this early stage of your tuition programme you will be concentrating on learning to put your model where you want to be in the sky relative to where you are standing on the ground. This will involve straight and level flight, simple banking turns, and recovery from such turns back to straight and level again.

You will also learn how to control the climb and sink rate of the model, using different throttle settings. Do not fall into the trap of thinking that your model has to be flying flat out at all times.

A model correctly trimmed for training flight should be set so that at about half throttle it flies straight and level, neither gaining nor losing altitude. This means that reduced throttle will cause the model to sink (less lift resulting from reduced forward air speed), whereas more throttle will cause it to climb (greater lift due to increased forward air speed).

Most of your training flights will be carried out at about half-throttle setting, which limits the speed of the model and is the most appropriate for learning. Too much forward speed at these early stages allows too little thinking time. Higher speeds can be used when you have learned to respond quickly to the control requirements of your model in any attitude and at any altitude.

As you put the model through different manoeuvres you will come to appreciate the need for changes of throttle input. The added drag and reduced lift created as the model changes its attitude and position in relation to the air passing over its surfaces will need to be compensated for by additional power from the engine.

Once you have mastered these basic skills and your instructor is happy that you are ready, you will be shown how to fly a number of accurate and specific manoeuvres that are recognizable as being totally controlled and well positioned in relation to your ground location.

NB: with three-function systems, for 'ailerons' read 'rudder'.

Clockwise (Right-Hand) Circle
This is the manoeuvre you are most likely to learn first when you fly from a field where the prevailing wind direction is west to east and you stand with your back to the sun. The

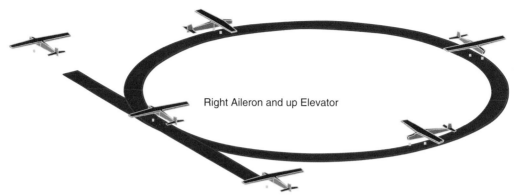
Right Aileron and up Elevator

Clockwise (right-hand) circuit.

model will be flying into wind and, as it passes directly in front of you, the application of a little right aileron followed by a small amount of up elevator will hold the model in a continuous right-hand turn.

If the turn has a tendency to tighten, release the aileron control a little and at the same time reduce the amount of up elevator. The natural stability of the model will cause the angle of bank to reduce hence the diameter of the circle will become larger.

The manoeuvre is fully controllable and with practice you will be able to keep the model in an almost perfect circle. Once the model comes round to where the circle started, you need to apply a little left aileron and release any up elevator you have been holding to straighten up its flight path. If you have done things right, the model should exit the circle at very near the same altitude at which it entered.

Providing you keep the circle large enough, it should not be necessary to increase motor speed, as the loss of lift due to the angle of bank will be very small. If the turn becomes tight, you will detect the nose beginning to drop. In this case you will need to apply a little more motor speed and slightly more up elevator to compensate for the loss of lift in the turn.

As with every manoeuvre you learn, unless you are very lucky or particularly gifted, the first attempts will be far from perfect. The answer is practice and more practice until you get it right every time.

Anti-Clockwise (Left-Hand) Circle

Set the model up flying towards you from left to right and, as it draws level with you, apply slight left aileron combined with a little up elevator. Hold or adjust these inputs to maintain a constant radius circle at constant altitude. As the model comes round the circle and is almost level with you again, apply slight right aileron and release the up elevator control.

You will normally learn this manoeuvre when the wind is coming from your right. Most instructors will teach structured manoeuvres from an approach into wind. This does not mean to say that at some future stage you will not need to practise these same turns out of a 'down-wind' approach.

It is important to be aware of the effect of the prevailing wind on these turns. In relatively still air, the effect will be small and will not have a very noticeable influence on the control inputs at the transmitter. The same cannot be said for days when the breeze is stronger. Flying into wind, the amount of aileron and elevator control input required to initiate the turn will be measurably less than the inputs required to maintain the turn as the model starts to negotiate the second

40

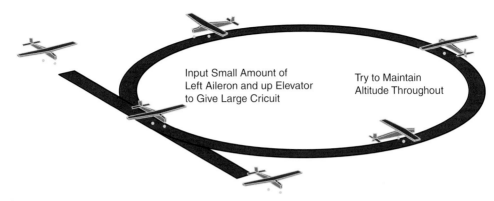

Input Small Amount of
Left Aileron and up Elevator
to Give Large Cricuit

Try to Maintain
Altitude Throughout

Anti-clockwise (left-hand) circuit.

half of the circle. It is essential to learn to handle these changes if you want to fly smooth manoeuvres while maintaining constant altitude.

Right-Hand Rectangular Circuit

This type of structured circuit is a precursor to attempting a landing approach. If you watch most display pilots you will see them perform this circuit as they set up the model for the landing. The whole arrangement has a very pleasing appearance and demonstrates accurate control at all stages.

Approaching into wind, fly the model past your position to a point about 50m (55 yards) up-wind of the pilot box. Apply some right aileron combined with up elevator. As the model reaches a position 90 degrees to its original flight path, apply a little opposite aileron and release the up elevator input.

Continue to fly straight and level for a further 50m (55 yards) before repeating the procedure. Fly a down-wind leg of about 95m (105 yards) and repeat the turn procedure again, using a little more aileron and up elevator to compensate for the wind factor.

Fly 45m (50 yards) straight and level before making the fourth turn. This should put the model virtually back on the trajectory of the original approach leg. Fly past your position straight and level into wind to complete the manoeuvre.

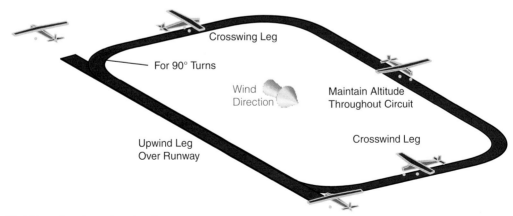

Crosswing Leg

For 90° Turns

Wind
Direction

Maintain Altitude
Throughout Circuit

Crosswind Leg

Upwind Leg
Over Runway

Crosswind Leg

Right-hand rectangular circuit.

You will notice the changes suggested for the distances to the final two turns. This is because down-wind turns and turns into wind usually take a little longer to complete.

The final turn into wind will test your appreciation of an apparent control input reversal. Although you will be observing the model approaching you about 50m (55 yards) down-wind, as you again select right stick for the ailerons the model will actually appear to be turning left into wind. This sometimes confuses the learner but it is absolutely essential to come to terms with the phenomenon. You will experience it even more closely when you start to fly the 'figure-of-eight' manoeuvre.

Left-Hand Rectangular Circuit

Again, the approach for this manoeuvre is into wind flying past your position for 50m (55 yards). Apply left aileron combined with a little gentle up elevator until you have negotiated a 90-degree turn away from yourself. Correct back to straight and level with a little right aileron and release the up elevator.

Fly 50m (55 yards), then repeat the first corner. Correct the turn and fly 95m (105 yards) straight and level. Repeat the 90-degree left turn again and fly 45m (50 yards) across wind toward your original approach position.

Once again you will experience the effect of control reversal as you apply left aileron for the fourth corner, and the model appears to make a right turn towards you into wind.

Practise this manoeuvre until you can maintain constant altitude throughout and your final turn into wind is as close to your original approach as possible.

Clockwise Procedure Turn

This is an interesting manoeuvre as it contains both right and left aileron inputs. Try to imagine drawing a large letter 'P' in the sky. Start by lining up the model for an approach into wind. As you reach a position about 15m (16 yards) from your position, apply some left aileron and slight up elevator. The model will turn away immediately in front of you if your timing is correct.

Apply right aileron and release the elevator input to fly straight and level away from you for about 30m (33 yards). Now apply right aileron and up elevator and hold the turn through 270 degrees (three-quarters of a circle), at which point you should be coming back on to your original approach line but in the opposite direction. Complete the manoeuvre by correcting the turn with left aileron and releasing the elevator input to fly past yourself at the same altitude as your initial approach, but in the opposite direction.

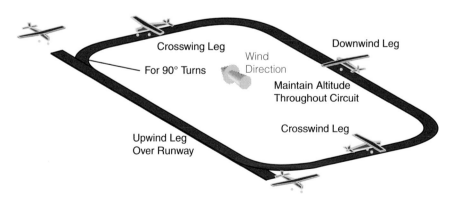

Counter-clockwise rectangular circuit.

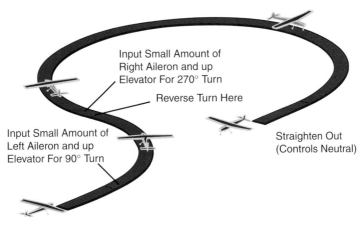

Input Small Amount of
Right Aileron and up
Elevator For 270° Turn

Reverse Turn Here

Input Small Amount of
Left Aileron and up
Elevator For 90° Turn

Straighten Out
(Controls Neutral)

Clockwise procedure turn.

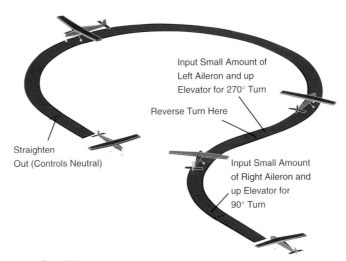

Input Small Amount of
Left Aileron and up
Elevator for 270° Turn

Reverse Turn Here

Straighten
Out (Controls Neutral)

Input Small Amount
of Right Aileron and
up Elevator for
90° Turn

Anti-clockwise procedure turn.

This is an attractive manoeuvre and demonstrates your ability to position your model precisely. Keep the circle part of the manoeuvre nice and wide to make the whole thing look good. Do not forget that you may need to increase the turn inputs a little as the model starts to pull through the down-wind section of the circle.

Anti-Clockwise Procedure Turn

This is the reverse of the clockwise version and commences with right aileron and eleva-tor followed by left aileron and elevator to complete the circle portion.

Figure-of-Eight

This uses all of the features of the previous manoeuvres, combining both circles and pro-cedure turns. You should ideally be standing 10 to 15m (11 to 16 yards) to the left of the intersection of the two circles.

Of course, when the wind is coming from the opposite direction the approach and turns will be reversed.

43

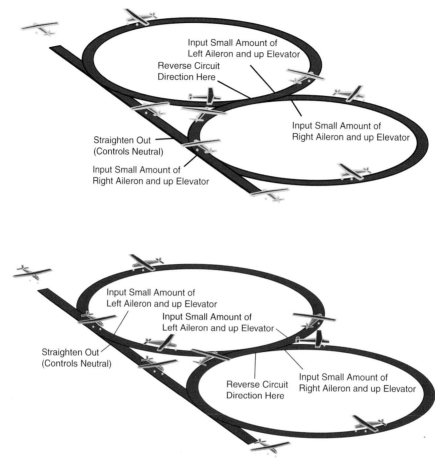

Figures of eight.

In all of the above examples, the test of good control is whether or not you can keep the circles consistent in size. In addition, the altitude at which you finish the manoeuvre should be the same as when you started it.

TAKE-OFF

When your instructor feels that you are ready and have the necessary aptitude, he will ask you to take off for yourself. This difficult task can be daunting for a beginner but, once it has been done for a first time, it will present less of a challenge the next time around.

The easiest way for a beginner to learn to take off is for the instructor to hold the model in its take-off position. The motor is run up to full speed and, when you are ready, the instructor releases the model. This minimizes the effect of gradually increasing the engine torque and propeller wash, both of which can tend to make the model yaw (swing) to the left.

If the model does tend to swing left, keep it on a straight heading using a little right rudder. Gradually reduce this rudder movement and, when the model has reached flying speed, ease in a small amount of up

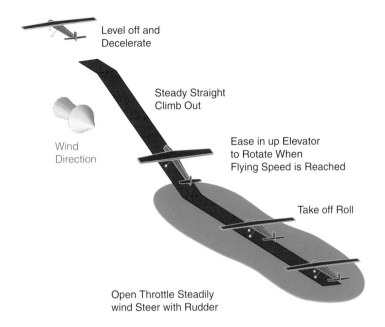

Level off and
Decelerate

Steady Straight
Climb Out

Wind
Direction

Ease in up Elevator
to Rotate When
Flying Speed is Reached

Take off Roll

Open Throttle Steadily
wind Steer with Rudder

Take-off.

elevator to rotate for take-off. If the model has been set up for straight and level flight with the motor at around half throttle, there may be no necessity to use up elevator as maximum rpm should put the model into a natural climb. Once the model has reached a safe altitude, reduce the throttle until the model adopts a straight and level attitude. Turn away from your flight line and do a few gentle circuits to get rid of excess adrenaline!

After two or three attempts at this, you should be ready to take the model off without the instructor's assistance. Taxi the model slowly out to the take-off point and turn it into wind. Reduce the glow motor to idle, or stop the electric motor, and compose yourself. Progressively increase the throttle, correct any swing if necessary with the rudder and suddenly you will find yourself airborne. Do not forget to fly out straight and level until you have sufficient altitude for your first safe turn away from the flight line.

It is important to avoid getting into the bad habit of turning in the direction that causes you to fly around yourself. Stand still and fly the model in circuits in front of you at all times. Never fly your model over other fliers and/or the pits area, car park, and so on.

LANDING

By the time you are ready to attempt a landing, you will be taking off and flying around safely. The only thing the instructor will be doing for you is landing and giving advice and constructive criticism.

As your ability and confidence increase, you will start to feel more comfortable flying the model at lower altitude. Having practised the rectangular circuits you will be ready to progress to adapting these circuits for landing approaches. In essence, the landing approach is a normal rectangular circuit during which you gradually lose altitude until, on the final

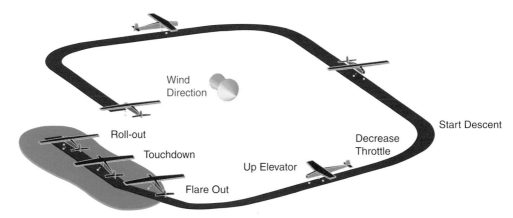

Landing – clockwise approach.

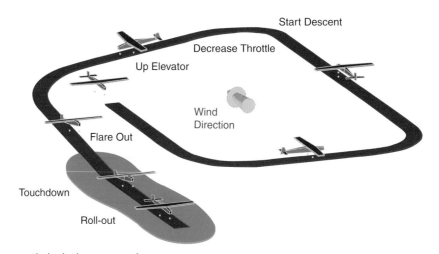

Landing – anti-clockwise approach.

turn into wind, you are at the correct height to place the model safely on the runway.

This will be explained and demonstrated to you by your instructor. You will start practising the approach and good or bad approaches will be pointed out to you. Try to locate visual markers or reference points around the flying field to help you make good consistent approaches.

You will be shown how to complete safe approach circuits. This involves reducing motor power on the down-wind and cross-wind legs so that the model drops to a lower level. Turning into wind, you will maintain a low fly past over the landing area. It is important to have full control during this manoeuvre and to be able to line the model up accurately and at a consistent safe height a few metres above the landing strip. You will then open the throttle to make a recovery climb out to a safe turning altitude, and repeat the circuit.

Practise these approaches until you are confident you can take the final step of cutting the power so that the model touches down safely. When you do finally cut the power for touchdown, watch that the nose does not drop too rapidly and be ready to feed in a small amount of up elevator to keep the nose from 'digging in'. Too much elevator will cause the model to stall, with possible damaging consequences.

This all sounds a bit traumatic but when you are ready your reactions should be quick enough to handle the situation. Your instructor, having gained experience with your model through previous landings, will be able to advise you on the best motor settings and elevator controls for successful landings.

SIMPLE AEROBATICS

Having progressed this far, your skills should be adequate for you to start considering a couple of the most basic aerobatic maneouvres: the loop and the roll.

The purpose of this manual is to help you master the basics of powered model-aircraft flight, not to teach you to do a full Aresti programme. The loop and the roll are, however, simple enough for the beginner to master once the basic horizontal flying challenges have been overcome.

Consult with your instructor and, providing he feels that you are ready for this progression, read on.

The Loop

'Open the throttle, pull up elevator and go over the top for a loop.' Most people think that is all there is to it, but that is far from true. Getting the loop circular and symmetrical is definitely not as easy as it would seem. It is subject to a number of external factors, including wind strength and direction, motor power, configuration of the model, and so on.

What exactly is involved? Ensuring that you have lots of altitude and that the wings are level, head straight into wind, open the throttle for full power and after a few seconds

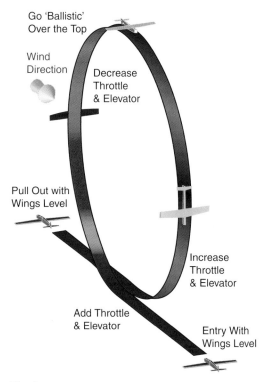

The Loop.

pull in almost full elevator. As the model passes through vertical, and approaches the top of the loop, cut throttle completely and release most of the elevator. The model will go over the top of the loop and start to drop its nose towards vertical. As the model passes the vertical (this time heading straight for the ground!), ease in up elevator and open up the throttle again to level out.

If you get it right, you should depart the loop flying straight and level at approximately the same height and position at which you entered it. It is most important to ensure that you have plenty of altitude before commencing your first attempts, just in case you get into difficulty.

With practice you will learn to make corrections for wind strength at different positions around the loop, much as you did when learning to fly circuits. In still air, the loop is relatively simple but in stronger breezes accurate loops are more difficult to master.

The Roll

The 'axial roll' (to give it its correct title) is pretty straightforward if you have masses of forward air speed and powerful control surfaces. Flying straight and level into wind, bang over full aileron control and hold it until the model assumes its upright position again. Let go the aileron stick and there you are – a perfect axial roll. At least, that would be the case if you were flying a high-speed ballistic-type aerobatic model, with enough speed and roll rate to complete the roll before the nose has the time to think about dropping.

You, however, are flying a trainer that does not possess these characteristics. If you tried this simple approach, your model would be on a downward trajectory towards the earth by the time it recovered to the upright attitude. This does not mean to say that you cannot fly an axial roll with your basic trainer; it just needs a little more attention to detail to make it happen.

What is the procedure? Ensure plenty of altitude for recovery in the event of disorientation or a mistake (same thing really!). Line up into wind, and increase motor speed to almost full throttle. This will start to lift the nose a little. Apply full left or right aileron input and the model will start to rotate about the roll axis, depending on which aileron input you selected.

As it approaches the inverted you will need to apply a little down elevator, which means pushing the elevator control stick away from you. Release this as soon as the model passes the inverted state and starts to roll upright again.

Once the model is in the straight and level attitude, release the aileron control input and reduce throttle back to half for level flight position.

It is important to practise the manoeuvre rolling both left and right. Avoid getting stuck in single rotation mode.

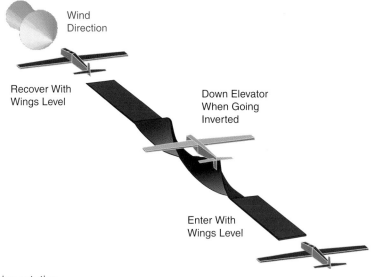

Roll – clockwise rotation.

As you become more proficient in this manoeuvre, try applying a little less aileron input so that the model rolls more slowly. You will notice that more down elevator is required for a longer period to maintain level flight in the inverted state.

ENGINE OUT OR MOTOR OFF FOR DEAD-STICK LANDING

So far, these instructions have assumed that everything is running smoothly and that your glow engine is not misbehaving. Occasionally, for no apparent reason, your engine may stop in mid-flight or when you throttle right back during a manoeuvre. You may have been flying for longer than you realize and simply run out of fuel, or your electric motor drive battery may be discharged.

Whatever the reason, you now have to get your model down safely and, ideally, if you are flying a safe radius of the take-off area, within a few metres of where you are standing. The most important consideration, of course, is to land it safely and without endangering the lives or equipment of your fellow fliers. Your club will have a recognized call to notify everyone of a stopped motor in flight. You need to be familiar with this call so that you can warn everyone of your need to land quickly and safely. Do not be afraid to shout it out loudly; everyone needs to be aware of what you are doing.

Unfortunately, when a motor stops it is often at the most inconvenient of moments, in a place where the model has no chance of recovering to the landing area in time. All you can hope to do in this instance is to line the model up into wind, altitude permitting, and control it into a gentle flair out. Do not attempt to hold the model off with the elevator as it will inevitably stall and crash.

If you are lucky enough to have the advantage of plenty of altitude, try to bring the model into a landing approach circuit. Try to judge the turns to lose the altitude for a normal landing on the runway in front of you. Your instructor should be able to advise you on the best points at which to turn.

Dead-stick approaches and landings should be an integral part of your training schedule. Discuss this with your instructor.

USING A FLIGHT SIMULATOR

An RC flight simulator computer program is a very good learning tool for any beginner, and advances in computer technology and software have resulted in a very high degree of realism. Although there is no substitute for actual flight training, virtual training at home can help teach the student pilot good hand and eye co-ordination. This kind of practice should improve the student's abilities at the flying field, as it can make reactions quicker. Less 'think time' means more time to correct for piloting errors.

Another advantage of flight simulators is that they extend the flying season for those who live in cooler climates. You can 'fly' all winter long without even leaving the house.

Several flight simulators are available and they all work roughly in the same way. The simulator presents an image on the computer screen of a model aircraft, which reacts to your control inputs. Some simulators come with a control box that looks very much like an RC transmitter; other systems provide an interface that lets you connect and use your own transmitter. You can choose from several types of model provided by the program, and you can even create new models or represent your own.

Most simulators offer a choice of flying environments. You can fly from a typical flying field, or the surface of Mars, or anywhere in between. You can adjust weather elements such as wind direction, cross-wind velocity and gusts. In this way, it is possible to make the flight simulation as easy or as difficult as you like.

By using a flight simulator, you can reduce the time it will take for you to learn how to fly your model. You can also continue to fly even when the weather is against you.

SUMMARY

The more time you can devote to flying as often as possible, the quicker you will progress. The more you fly, the sooner the day will come when your instructor will allow you to attempt that first landing. Your instructor must be absolutely sure that you are ready for this step. This is a critical time for the instructor since he must react quickly if you make a mistake. It may take you several attempts before you actually set the model down on the runway. Even then, it might bounce through lack of control and seem to be flying again. If this happens, you must continue to control the model all the way to the point when it stops rolling.

After what may seem like an eternity, the day will come when your instructor is satisfied that you are proficient enough in your flying skills to fly solo. This can be equally harrowing and exhilarating. You may feel that you have finally reached your goal but this is only the beginning. Now the fun really starts, as you spend hour after hour practising and developing your skills. Do remember that this is only the first stage in your progression to becoming a fully competent model pilot. There is still a long way to go before you reach the standard of your instructor.

Treat your model with respect, follow the simple basic guidelines and there is no reason why, given enough time and practice, you should not eventually become as competent as those with the skills you envy and admire.

This is also the stage at which you may feel ready to progress to a new model with more aerobatic potential. Do not, however, be tempted to splash out immediately on a WW2 fighter type, an out-and-out aerobat, 3D machine or 'turn it inside out' fun-fly machine; there will be plenty of time for those later. Consider instead a somewhat more advanced trainer type with mid- or low-wing configuration. This will be marginally more aerobatic but will still have a good measure of natural stability.

There are a good number of attractive designs to take you through this intermediate stage en route to more advanced flying, including some interesting scale or semi-scale models of mid-war and modern civil types. Get the opinion of your instructor and look at what other post-student grade members are flying before making your final choice.

Whatever your choice, go out and enjoy your new-found skills and help promote this wonderful hobby safely.

This low-wing trainer makes an ideal follow-on from the basic high-wing trainer and can use the same engine/radio combination.

A typical 'jet-style' low-wing model makes a suitable introduction to more advanced sport aerobatics.

Two planes for the more advanced pilot wishing to develop 3D-style flying skills.

The very popular Funtana design, for familiarization with F3A aerobatics to FAI and Aresti schedules.

The ultimate introduction to large-scale aerobatics, powered by a 60cc petrol engine for F3M or IMAC scale contests.

CHAPTER 5
RESOURCES

EQUIPMENT REQUIREMENTS

Glow Models

The equipment required to get a trainer off the ground can be relatively inexpensive compared to the cost of the other components. A few basic items will get a beginner into the air and learning to fly, but there are additional items that can be added to make the job a lot easier.

The minimum equipment list is as follows:

- glow-plug driver – clip-on battery for supplying power to glow plug
- chicken stick – used for flicking prop to start engine
- fuel (in mixture recommended by engine manufacturer)
- fuel squeeze bottle, to transfer fuel to model tank
- four-way wrench, with sizes to fit glow plug, prop nut, and so on
- tool box suitable for carrying other equipment

The cost of these items will vary depending on the brand and the supplier. An assortment of screwdrivers, pliers, and allen keys or wrenches may also be needed, to carry out maintenance at the field.

An optimum equipment list might look something like the following:

- starter – battery -powered motor for starting model engine
- glow plug connector – clip-on battery connector for supplying power to glow plug
- power distribution panel, for distributing power from a field battery to starter, glow plug connector, and so on
- field battery – small 12-volt wet or gel cell battery
- fuel (in mixture recommended by engine manufacturer
- fuel pump, to transfer fuel to model tank;
- four-way wrench, with sizes to fit glow plug, prop nut, and so on
- field box – tool box specifically designed for carrying model field equipment

Again, the cost will vary depending on the brand and where you buy them. Field box kits are available at a wide range of prices but may also be built from readily available materials. Plans are available for either a simple field box that will fit the needs of a beginner or for a basic necessities field box for a beginner who wants something a little more sophisticated. As before, an assortment of screwdrivers, pliers, spanners, and allen wrenches may also be needed for ongoing maintenance.

Electric Models

The minimum equipment required for the operation of electric models will be a tool box for carrying bits and pieces, as well as an assortment of screwdrivers, pliers, and allen keys or wrenches.

As you gain more experience, you might consider acquiring a field box, which is specifically designed for carrying model field equipment. Another addition might be a power measurement device – a wattmeter or, as an absolute minimum, a multi-meter capable of measuring the maximum current drawn by your motor.

PRE-FLIGHT CHECKS

When your model is ready to fly, it should be thoroughly checked over by someone who has done a lot of building and flying. Every detail of set-up and connection should be gone over in detail. If your instructor seems reluctant to spend this much time checking your plane, find a new instructor! The importance of this pre-flight check cannot be over-emphasized. Many models are lost due to a simple oversight that could have been caught by a pre-flight check.

The following features should be checked thoroughly:

- Weight – is the model too heavy?
- Balance – is the centre of gravity (fore and aft) within the range shown on the plans? Is the model balanced side to side? (right and left wings of equal weight)
- Alignment – are all flying surfaces at the proper angle relative to each other? Are there any twists in the wings (apart from built in wash-in or wash-out)?
- Are all control surfaces securely attached? (Are the hinges glued, not just pushed in?)
- Are the control throws set to the correct direction and amount? (This is normally indicated in the plans.)
- Have all control linkages been checked to make sure they are secure?
- Are all snap-links (clevises) closed and keepers fitted?
- Have snap-links been used on the servo end? (They are more likely to come loose when used on the servo.)

- Have all screws been attached to servo horns?
- Glow motor – has the engine been thoroughly tested? Are all engine screws tight? Has the engine been run up at full throttle with the plane's nose straight up in the air? (This is to ensure that it will not stall when full power is applied on climb out.) Is the fuel tank level with the flying attitude of the plane? Is the carburettor at the same height as the fuel tank (not above it)? Is the fuel tank clunk in the proper position and moving freely?
- Electric motor, ESC and battery – has the motor been thoroughly tested and run in? Are all the mountings tight? Is the flight battery fully charged? Has the maximum current drain been checked to be within safe limits? Is the battery pack securely fastened in place?
- Radio – has a full range check been performed? Has the flight pack charge been checked with a voltmeter? Have the receiver and battery been protected from vibration and shock? Is the receiver's antenna fully extended and not placed within a fuselage with any sort of metallic covering?

After any repair, the checklist should be gone through again, with particular attention to the areas that were worked on.

Before *every* flight, the following checks should be carried out:

- use a voltmeter to ensure there is enough charge in the receiver flight pack
- check the control throw direction for all surfaces. It is very easy to do a repair or radio adjustment and forget to switch these
- start the motor and test the entire speed range. Run your glow motor at full throttle with its nose in the air for 15 seconds or so to ensure there is no evidence of fuel

starvation. Should it tend to slow, open the fuel control needle valve a few notches until it regains its full running speed;

- always remember that, with model aircraft, take-offs are optional, landings are mandatory!

RC PROPELLER SAFETY

There are a number of basic guidelines that relate to RC propellers:

- Always adhere to your engine manufacturer's recommendations for size and pitch.
- Balance RC propellers before using. This is a must for safety and best performance.
- White painted propeller tips have a more scale appearance and can be seen.
- Always use a 'chicken stick' or other approved device for starting. *No hands!*
- Keep yourself and others, especially their hands, away from the path of rotating blades.
- Make carburettor adjustments from behind the prop where possible or with the engine at low revs.
- Check for objects that can be picked up and blown back from below and in front of the prop.
- Make sure nothing can fall from your pockets into rotating blades.

- When running a glow engine, be sure the attaching cable and clip cannot tangle in prop.
- *Never* try to recondition or re-use a damaged, nicked or bent propeller.
- Do *not* buy used propellers!

KNOWING YOUR GLOW ENGINE

How a Two-Stroke Engine Works

Most glow-powered trainers are flown using a two-stroke engine, but how exactly do they work?

Air is drawn in through the carburettor barrel, where it is mixed with the fuel before entering the intake port. The piston is on the down stroke so the mixture is drawn up the bypass ports into the combustion chamber. As the piston travels upwards, it compresses the mixture. The pressure reaches a point where the glow plug ignites the mixture and forces the piston back down the cylinder, opening the exhaust port, expelling the exhaust gases and surplus oil. The piston starts to rise again, forcing a new fuel/air mixture charge into the combustion chamber.

Not all of the expanding exhaust gases can pass through the muffler at once. Some of it will stay in the muffler as the next cycle begins. This retained exhaust gas causes a back pressure that helps keep the new charge

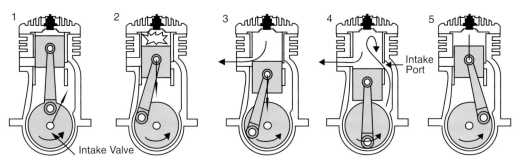

Two-stroke cycle.

of unburned mixture from entering the combustion chamber, blowing over the top of the piston and out through the exhaust. This results in better fuel economy.

Timing is achieved by several factors: glow plug heat, port locations, crankshaft design and length of stroke (length the piston travels up and down). If any one of these is out of tolerance, this will cause ignition of the fuel/air mixture before the piston reaches top dead centre. This phenomenon is called 'detonation' or 'pre-ignition'.

Breaking in Your Engine

The object of breaking in or running in an engine is to get the engine to the point at which all the rubbing surfaces are perfectly mated to each other, at all the temperatures that are likely to be attained, while causing as little wear to the engine as possible.

The benefits of doing this properly are that the engine will be 'better' throughout its life. That life will also be extended. If you can get hold of one, use an old (but working) glow plug when first running in your engine. Often, minute pieces of metal from the running-in process or swarf left from manufacturing can destroy a glow plug in seconds.

Run the engine very rich and lightly loaded at first. Gradually increase the amount of load on the engine, at the same time gradually increasing the temperature that the engine is allowed to reach through careful adjustment of the main needle valve. Spread this gradual process over approximately the first half-hour of the engine's life. It should then be ready for its first full-speed run.

During all running of new engines, the setting should be on the rich side of peak power. Try to run the engine in for this period with the throttle fully open.

The difference between a reliable engine and a troublesome one is very often how it is treated in the first 15 minutes of its life!

Ringed Engines

Most manufacturers recommend either castor-based fuels or synthetic oil-based fuels with the addition of castor for the first run or runs.

The first tankful should be run absolutely soggy-rich, leaving the glow-plug lead attached if necessary to keep the engine running. Make these first runs short – one-half to one minute – with a few minutes' cooling-down time between each one. A good number of these heat cycles will make the metal 'set' and speed up the final fit of the components. Rich mixtures and short runs prevent the temperature from rising too much. Any debris that forms will be washed away by the excess fuel and oil.

Refill the tank and set the main fuel needle to give a very fast four-stroke with just the occasional hint of two-stroking. Allow the engine to run for 30 seconds and then stop for a two-minute cooling period. Check the tightness of all bolts. Start the engine again for 30 seconds then allow it to cool again. Gradually increase the duration of the full-throttle runs, unless the engine shows a tendency to bind. Binding will cause the engine to labour and fail to maintain a steady rpm.

At the end of two tankfuls you can lean the engine out to the point where it is on the verge of two-stroking and four-stroking and go fly. Reduce throttle from time to time to allow the engine to cool a bit. Keep this up for about 4 litres of fuel.

By this time, the engine should be running steadily, with no tendency for the rpm to fluctuate up or down. At this point the engine can be leaned further so that maximum power is achieved. Always back off the needle a bit (one or two 'clicks' on the needle should be enough) until a clear drop in rpm can be detected. This should be the normal setting for longevity and strong running in the air. During flight, the engine will lean out a bit, so you will be on the safe side of disaster with this setting.

This might seem a long-winded process but it is necessary to get the best surface finish with the least wear inside your precious engine.

Everything needs to be done in small and gradual steps so that the rubbing surfaces can mate at gradually increasing pressures. To complicate this further, the component parts of the engine change shape as temperatures are increased. For example, the cylinder and piston are round and parallel-sided when made. As the engine warms up, the top half of the cylinder gets hotter than the bottom half and so expands unevenly; in addition, the exhaust side of the liner runs hotter than the fuel transfer side.

To add to the problem, the front of the engine being cooled by the airflow does not heat up as much as the rear of the engine. As a consequence, the liner will be anything but perfectly round and parallel when thoroughly hot.

These factors are the reason why a well run-in engine has a bit less compression during starting than a new engine.

Similar stresses affect the piston and ring. The ring changes its length depending on temperature and is also going up and down a bore that is no longer round or parallel-sided. At the same time, it is taken through this operation by a piston that gets hotter at its head, where it is in contact with the burning fuel mixture. The diameter of the head is bigger than the walls, the exhaust side of the piston is hotter than the transfer side, so the piston is no longer round nor parallel-sided.

All these distortions vary according to the temperature of the engine. The running-in process will give the engine the necessary opportunity to make the mating working surfaces suitable for every condition.

At various intervals during the running-in process (say, every 5–10 minutes), check that all screws and bolts remain tight. If you have to tighten any cylinder head bolts, do so a little at a time and always in diagonal rotation. It is possible that the glow plug will have been affected by small metal particles fired at it during running in. If you are unsure of its condition, change it and keep the old one for running in only, or throw it away.

ABC Engines

An ABC engine is one with special liner and piston metallurgy – the piston is aluminium (A), the liner is brass (B), and the brass is chrome-plated (C). Generally (but not always) these are performance-oriented engines.

Brass expands more than aluminium, so when an ABC engine is warmed up, the top of the liner (brass) will expand more than the piston (aluminium). In a normal engine, as working temperature was reached, the piston seal would not be very satisfactory. To compensate for this difference, manufacturers make the liner and piston the correct sizes for when the engine is hot. This means that when the engine is cold the piston is a very tight fit at the top of the liner. Some engines are so tight they make a light groaning noise when forced over top dead centre (or 'TDC', that is, the point at which the piston is at the very top of its travel).

Never turn a new ABC engine over slowly, especially when still lubricated by the original preserving oil with which it was shipped. Slight, but immediate damage will be caused to the top part of the piston fit, because the surfaces are still rough.

Running In

These engines require only a relatively small amount of running in. The cylinder temperature needs to be raised to full working temperature as quickly as possible, to avoid excessive piston wear; the fit at lower temperatures is very tight. It is acceptable to fly an ABC straight from the box, using a rich setting so that it occasionally drops back to four stroking, but the 15-minute rule still applies. A good period of running in, preferably on a test stand, will be well worthwhile. (The test stand is a handy tool that may be worth the investment longer term; most will cope with 2cc–30cc engines.) It is a good idea to use a fuel with an extra 5 per cent of oil above a normal fuel mixture. Run the first tank (say, 1–2 minutes) at a quarter-throttle position, with the engine on a rich two-stroke setting, ensuring that you can still feel unused oil exiting the silencer on your fingertips. The engine may have been in its box for quite a long time, and this will nicely lubricate all the moving parts. Allow the engine to cool, then run it for 1–2 minutes at half-throttle. For the next 3–4 minutes, it should be run with the throttle wide open, again with unused oil exiting the silencer, but with a stronger rpm setting (to bed in the moving parts). Complete the running in, either on the test stand or in the model, until the engine is capable of holding full rpm without faltering.

During the first couple of flights, run the engine in short cycles of approximately 30 seconds at full speed, then drop back to one-third speed for 5 to 10 seconds. This will keep the cylinder temperature up and the slow running allows time for any hot spots to cool down a little. For the next four or five flights, use the engine normally, but keep it slightly rich (just two or three clicks). After that, normal manufacturer's recommended fuel can be used.

Setting the Main Needle Valve
This sets maximum power and controls the running temperature of the engine. These two factors not only determine the length of the engine's life, but also influence the life of the glow plug and the overall reliability of the engine. An engine will rarely cut out in flight when it is set slightly too rich, but it often will when set too lean.

It takes five minutes or so to learn the drill for correct needle valve setting, and it is well worth taking the trouble for the long-term benefits gained.

ABC engines start best on low throttle settings. Once the engine is running, open the throttle fully and set the engine slightly rich so that it is just four-stroking. Let the engine warm through thoroughly at top speed for a few moments before re-adjusting the needle so that the engine is just off four-stroking, and running smoothly.

Now further lean out of the mixture until the rpm increases to maximum. From this established point richen up slowly again until a small but definite drop in rpm is noticed, but the engine is still two-stroking smoothly. Lift the nose of the model up vertically and if the engine rpm increases back to maximum then you should have a good flight setting. Should the model have a tendency to go rich or lean in flight, an extra allowance will have to be made for this on the final setting.

Your aim must be to achieve maximum power from the engine when it is needed most, either when the model is climbing or when it is turning sharply. At the same time, the setting should provide sweet and cool running during level flight.

Glow-plug engines keep running because the heat of compression and the catalytic action of the glowing plug material on the methanol mixture cause the charge in the cylinder to ignite at the correct moment. This catalytic action also keeps the plug glowing. Sometimes an engine will start without adding power to the plug after it has been stopped for several minutes. The whole system is very temperature-dependant and under certain circumstances requires no glow or injection of fuel to set it off, just the correct combination of conditions.

If an engine is set lean for maximum rpm at the start of a tankful of fuel, anything that reduces the amount of the fuel through the needle valve will make the engine run excessively lean. Some engines will refuse to continue running in this condition. The majority will continue to run to some degree, but at reduced rpm, reduced power and extremely hot, causing premature wear and/or failure.

The most common factor in reducing fuel pressure is the increased air volume and diminishing fuel level in the tank as it is used up. The pressure, seen by the needle valve, gradually reduces and the air/fuel mixture gets progressively leaner as the flight continues. An engine that has started set in a lean condition eventually progresses into an over-lean condition, and may possibly cut out, suffer from overheating and incur internal damage.

The extra stresses caused by overheating and excess pressures may cause an engine to wear out more rapidly than necessary. In addition, running an engine lean on a regular basis may result in very early bearing failure; if it happens to be the con-rod that gives up first, the resultant damage can be very expensive.

Setting the Low Speed or Idle Setting
As the throttle is closed it not only reduces the amount of fuel entering the carburettor, but also lets less air through into the engine. To keep the fuel/air mixture within combustible limits the fuel flow ratio has to be altered; it is too fussy to leave to chance. Most

Idle setting adjustment screw.

manufacturers have opted for a two-needle configuration, or something that works in a similar manner.

Start the engine and warm it up, making sure the main needle is properly set. Leave the glow-plug lead connected, to energize the plug, and slow the engine down by gradually closing the throttle until the engine starts to run unevenly. Adjust the slow run needle to give smoothest running characteristics just a little on the rich side of the fastest setting you can achieve.

Having made this adjustment, slow the engine further until it runs unevenly again, then adjust the slow needle once more until the engine runs smoothly. Continue this step-by-step procedure until the desired tick-over has been reached. At this point the throttle barrel should be barely 1mm open.

Now remove the plug lead and repeat the whole process. If the engine cuts dead in the middle of adjustments it is usually because it is too lean. You may need to set the slow running needle a click richer at each adjustment (an eighth to a quarter turn). With the engine at a slow tick-over, check that it will pick up properly. Open the throttle to full speed with a smooth sweep, without slamming the control stick hard forwards.

Troubleshooting:

1. The engine picks up but splutters a little whilst doing so – the low-speed needle is set a little rich.
2. The engine appears to miss and then picks up – the low speed needle is slightly lean.
3. The engine cuts dead when the throttle is opened – the low speed needle is set too lean; richen the low speed needle a quarter turn and try again, adjusting in small increments.
4. The engine starts to pick up pretty well and then cuts at about one-third speed or so – try opening the main needle two or three clicks.

There is often a compromise to get the low speed, mid-range, top speed and pick-up to a useable state. Usually, the carburettor has to be set a little richer than might be considered ideal. This is not really such a bad thing as a rich mixture assures longevity for the engine, and seldom causes the engine to stop, unless it is extreme.

Air bleed carbs work like 'twin needle' carbs, although they are not normally quite as accurate at setting the low speed air/fuel mixture. Richen the setting by screwing the needle (or bolt) in. To lean the setting, turn the needle (or bolt) out.

The Pinch Test

Pinch the fuel line between tank and carburettor and observe whether the engine speeds up. If it does, it is on the rich side of the optimum adjustment. The extent to which it speeds up indicates how close you are:

1. If it speeds up considerably, the setting is rich.
2. If it speeds up just a little, the setting is just about correct.
3. If it does not speed up at all, the engine is on the point of going lean.
4. If it slows down, the setting is lean.

This test causes a temporary starvation of fuel, and is a reliable test for the engine being too lean. The ideal setting is when, at full throttle, quickly pinching the fuel supply line causes the engine momentarily to increase its rpm before starting to die. If it starts to die immediately, then it is already too lean and should be adjusted for a richer setting.

KNOWING YOUR ELECTRIC MOTOR

As this is a guide to learning to fly rather than a technical manual, it cannot be the ultimate resource on electric motor technology. It is,

Typical wiring arrangement for a brushed motor.

however, worthwhile giving a simple explanation of what makes your motor work, as well as advice on the care and preparation of motors for flight, including simple maintenance and precautions you can take to prolong their life.

Unlike glow engines, electric motors are far more flexible in their ability to power models of different weights and sizes. This is because, within reason, the more volts you provide, the more current is drawn and, the bigger the propeller or coarser the propeller pitch you use, the more power the motor produces. Glow engines are fairly inflexible in this respect. The more they are loaded, the slower the rpm, with a consequent reduction in power and performance. Electric motors, however, will try to maintain optimum rpm by drawing more current from the battery at the expense of duration and greater heat energy loss.

Electrical power (watts) output is a function of the potential energy (volts) of the battery multiplied by the current (amps) drawn by the motor, or, shown as a formula:

$$\text{Watts (W)} = \text{Volts (V)} \times \text{Amps (A)}$$

Very simply, therefore, if the current is increased by fitting a larger propeller (additional load), the amount of watts will increase, providing more energy to power the model but at the expense of motor run time because the battery will be drained more quickly.

If another cell is added to a battery pack the voltage will increase, the motor and propeller will spin more quickly causing the current to increase, again draining the battery pack more quickly and reducing flying time.

Whatever you do that increases load on the motor and/or power consumption, current will increase at the expense of run time. This is because current increases by the following factors:

- added battery voltage ^{2};
- increased propeller diameter ^{4};
- propeller pitch ^{3}.
- ($^$ = to the power of)

Even if they have an understanding of the theory, most beginners will use the motor and battery combination provided by the kit manufacturer or recommended by them. Those brave enough to attempt a glow to electric conversion would be well advised to consult an expert in electric flight, their local model supplier, the internet or someone in their club who is conversant with these matters.

Running In

In order to prolong the life of a brushed motor, it is vital to run it in. This ensures that the square-ended carbon brushes contour themselves to the rounded shape of the commutator, increasing the area of contact and minimizing the amount of arcing that can occur. (This procedure is unnecessary with brushless motors as there are no rubbing contact points.)

For the simplest method of running in, buy two 1.5-volt dry 'D' cells, obtain or construct a cheap battery holder to connect the batteries in series (end to end) and fit small spade connectors or crocodile clips to the wires. With no propeller fitted, clip the leads to the motor and allow it to run the batteries completely flat. Do not forget to connect the leads in reverse so that your motor runs in 'backwards' or the 'wrong' way if you are going to be using a single-stage gearbox. For a belt-driven gearbox the motor will run in normal rotation.

Lubrication

If your motor is of the type that has ball races at either end of the output shaft, and they are not sealed, you need to apply a little Teflon or silicone grease occasionally.

Plain bearing motors also benefit from the application of a little light oil, of the type used for sewing machines. Only the smallest spot is required on the shaft where it emerges from the can. Gearboxes also need to be lubricated regularly with a little Teflon or silicone grease on the teeth. If your gears are plastic, or a combination of metal and plastic, ensure the lubricant you use is plastic-friendly. The output shafts of the gearbox should be lubricated in the same way as the motor.

Power Considerations

Apart from these simple basic precautions there is not a great deal more you can do to protect or maintain your motor. Just be sure that the current being drawn from the battery is not exceeding the manufacturer's recommended value. How do you determine whether your motor is running within safe parameters? Motors, ESCs and batteries all have constraints on their safe operating conditions.

If you overload a glow engine, or supply it with fuel containing insufficient oil, it is unlikely to do anything worse than destroy itself by seizing up. Electric flight systems, however, can not only self-destruct but also often react by producing heat, sparks, flames and a model fireball. It is therefore essential to know whether your power train is functioning well within its design parameters.

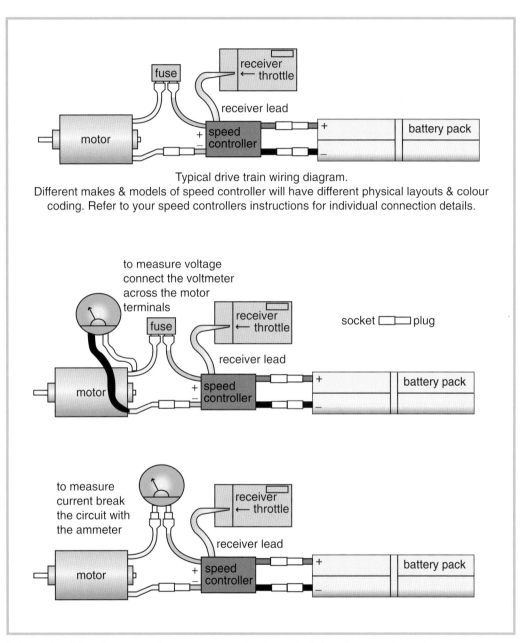

Typical drive train wiring diagram.
Different makes & models of speed controller will have different physical layouts & colour coding. Refer to your speed controllers instructions for individual connection details.

Drive train wiring diagram and measurement of voltage (volts) and current (amps).

The critical factors in this equation are the current being drawn, the capability of the batteries to supply this drain, and the ability of the ESC and motor windings to handle the current.

You need to be able to measure the three critical values of voltage, current and power being used by your system. There are a number of combined ammeter/wattmeters on the market specifically designed for model applications. If you are considering electric power as your main model propulsion method for future projects, you would be strongly recommended to invest in such a tool. You will find it indispensable in the future. Most of these devices have the capacity to measure four motor parameters: voltage (volts), current (amps), power (watts) and the capacity both going into (during charging) and coming out of the battery (measured in amps, ampere-hours, or Ah).

When using a brushed motor it is advisable to fit a fuse between the motor and the ESC, usually in the positive lead. The most convenient are the automotive blade fuses sold by auto spares centres. Fit two spade connectors in the positive line to hold your fuse.

The rating of this fuse will depend on the size of motor and the current rating. As a general rule of thumb, 10 amps for a 400 motor and 20 amps for a 600 motor are appropriate. If you are going to use a brushless motor, consult the manufacturer's rating and your current checks using the wattmeter. Fit a fuse capable of delivering the necessary maximum short-burst current requirements.

Electronic Speed Controller (ESC)

Without an ESC, the only option you would have to control your motor would be a very basic ON/OFF switch. This is fine if you are not looking to become a serious model pilot and just wish to play with the flying-toy type of aircraft. If you want to progress to more complex flying techniques, including even the most basic aerobatics, you will need full control over the speed and power of your motor. The answer is an ESC placed between batteries and motor. This takes the place of the throttle servo on a model powered by a glow engine. It gives you total proportional control over the rpm of your motor as well as the ability to switch it on and off either during flight, or at take-off or landing.

For the size of motor used on most trainer-type aircraft the ESC will also incorporate a battery elimination circuit (BEC). This is highly desirable for this type of model as it eliminates the necessity for a separate receiver battery. Weight considerations are very important for electric-powered models so anything you can do to eliminate additional payload will be well rewarded in the long term.

The BEC drops the full voltage of the motor drive battery down to a suitable level for safe operation of your receiver. It also protects the receiver from any rapid voltage fluctuations resulting from sudden or excessive motor loads, and so on. It also cuts off the supply to the motor before the battery voltage drops below a safe level for the receiver to function safely. As a consequence, you always have sufficient power to enable you to make a dead-stick landing if you overrun your flight time.

The type of ESC you use will depend on whether your motor is a brushed type or brushless. An ESC for a brushed motor will not work with a brushless motor. The brushed type only requires the ESC to vary the voltage level seen across the motor commutator.

Brushless motors work on a pulsed voltage system where the length and frequency of the individual pulses determine the speed of the motor in rpm. This is a more complex electronic function requiring a more sophisticated circuit. Make sure you buy the right one!

Batteries and Battery Care

Flight packs are made up from a number of individual cells soldered or welded together in

Size comparison of NiMh and LiPoly batteries.

series. The overall voltage will be the sum of all of the individual cell voltages. For example, Nicad (nickel cadmium) and NiMh (nickel metal hydride) batteries have a cell voltage of 1.2 volts each. If six of these are joined together in series (end to end, + to –) the result is a pack with combined voltage of $6 \times 1.2 = 7.2$ volts.

The current delivery capability is determined by the individual cell capacity only. This means that, no matter how many cells are joined end to end, the current capacity will never be greater than the single cell capacity. Fortunately, cells are available in many capacities, varying from around 250mAh (milliamp/hour) to 3000mAh. (The mAh rating indicates how many milliamps the cell is capable of delivering for an hour continuously.)

It is true that the bigger the capacity you use the more power you get, but, of course, the greater the cell capacity, the larger and heavier the pack will be – a six-cell pack of 3000mAh cells will weigh much more than a 1200mAh six-cell pack. At worst, this additional weight could render your model incapable of flight; at best, it will be a very difficult model to fly because of the high wing loading.

There is always a trade off between watts per pound, wing loading and duration:

- Watts per pound determines the model's performance capability.
- Wing loading, measured in g/sq dm (grams per square decimetre) or lb/sq ft (pounds per square foot) of wing area, determines its ease of handling.
- Duration is determined by the power drain on the battery required to keep the model airborne.

Lithium-Ion and Lithium-Polymer (Li-Poly) cells are different. They have a single cell voltage of 3.7 volts nominally. Fully charged, this can be as high as 4.2 volts. These are usually connected either two or three in series giving nominal pack voltages of 7.4 volts (2 series) or 11.1 volts (3 series). Because these cells are much lighter in weight than Nicad and NiMh, they can be 'ganged' into parallel packs – for example, 2S2P (2 series × 2 parallel = 4 cells) or 3S2P (3 series × 2 parallel = 6 cells) – for higher current delivery capability without excessive weight penalty.

In using these batteries, there is always a temptation to keep increasing the load on them in order to extract more performance from your model. They will keep trying to give you extra performance, but the penalty of drawing excessive current is overheating, to the point at which they could explode or burst into flames. Trying to prove this point could cost you your model!

The most important thing to remember is that everything is controlled by the safe working envelope of the motor/ESC/battery combination.

Your flight packs should be stored in the discharged state in which they were left after the last flight. Re-charge them only when you need to fly with them. Treat them with respect, as a fully charged battery pack is capable of causing considerable damage if short-circuited.

When charging your batteries follow the manufacturer's guidelines exactly to maximize their life expectancy. Treat every part of your power system with respect and care and it will reward you with many happy hours of flying.

QUICK-REFERENCE BEGINNER'S TIPS

- Roll-test steering in a driveway or car park. If model does not roll straight at home, it will not roll straight on a runway. Set control to least sensitive position.
- Put small marks at CoG (centre of gravity) on wing to indicate balance location; easy to check at field.
- Balancing laterally (side to side) will help aircraft track better in manoeuvres. Hold at spinner and tail. Add wingtip weight as necessary.
- Check receiver battery every two to three flights. Make chart of time flown against voltage drop. Do not operate below recommended voltage level.
- Always turn on transmitter first, receiver second. Always turn off receiver first, transmitter second.
- Range check system before first flight every time out, with engine running at both idle and full throttle.
- When using buddy-box system, make sure both boxes are set identical. Never turn buddy-box power 'ON'!
- Remove transmitter neck straps when starting engines.
- If you do not have a starter, at least use a 'chicken stick' to start glow engine. Do not hit it against the propeller; start flick with stick touching propeller.
- Never jamb a running starter on to the spinner. Back up propeller to a position just after top-dead-centre, and place starter cone against spinner before turning on.

- When starting glow engine, look at your watch and keep track of time. After flight, check fuel level to assess maximum available flight time.
- Do not reach over propeller to adjust needle valve – do it from rear of propeller. Do not position yourself (or others) to the side of a rotating blade. It could fail on run-up or kick up debris.
- Taxi while holding 'up elevator'.
- Always fly with a co-pilot/spotter.
- Never practise manoeuvres at low altitude. Fly two to three mistakes above ground.
- When trimming an aircraft in flight, trim only until it stops incorrect movement.
- Most trainer aircraft will recover from unusual attitudes (mistakes) by killing power and pulling up elevator (depending on altitude). Be ready to level out and apply power.
- Remember, unless you are 'dead stick', you do not have to land. If not right, go around. It is much easier, and safer, to do it again rather than try to salvage a bad approach.
- If you get nervous for any reason, climb out and do some simple circuits over the field. When you have calmed down, try again. Take your time.
- Do not fly too far away from yourself; it is easy to get disorientated, especially when the sun is low on the horizon and the aircraft becomes a silhouette.
- Install larger wheels on your trainer to make taxiing in grass easier; improve your visual orientation in the air; improve your landings (gear will not bend as easily).
- Maintain your flight path. Do not make any erratic manoeuvres to avoid faster, more manoeuvrable overtaking aircraft. It is their responsibility to avoid you. Do make a conscientious effort not to be a hazard either.

- If it is obvious that you are going to crash, kill the power to minimize damage.
- If for any reason your aircraft is in trouble and headed for the pit area or spectators, do your best to kill the power and ditch it. Do not try to save it. Planes are cheaper than people.
- If your aircraft does go down in a field or trees, do not move until you have taken note of where you are standing, and picked a far distance reference point or object. Follow a straight line in your search and rescue effort.
- If you are searching in the trees, listen for glow-powered aircraft overhead to orient yourself to the flight line and runway.
- When recovering a crashed aircraft, be sure to pick up every last part, piece and splinter, in case you decide to rebuild it after the shock wears off. Little pieces can be glued together to make templates to create replacement parts.
- If you have adjusted the elevator trim to compensate for lower fuel weight in your glow model during the later part of the flight, when you land, immediately reset the elevator trim to the 'full fuel tank' position. You probably won't remember until you are about 10 feet off the ground on the next take-off and struggling to keep your model airborne!
- Even long after you've gone solo, never be afraid to ask for additional help or instruction. It's never too late to learn!

GLOSSARY

AMA (Academy of Model Aeronautics)   US governing body for model-aircraft activities.

ABC   type of engine in which the piston and cylinder liner use a combination of aluminium, brass and chrome to give maximum compression at all temperatures, resulting from the equal expansion rate of the three metals.

Aerial   used to radiate the signal from the transmitter (Tx) and to receive the signal on the receiver (Rx).

Aerobatic trainer   training model with more advanced airfoils, more power, greater control movements and less inherent stability than a basic trainer.

Aerobatic model   model capable of performing advanced manoeuvres in the air.

Aerodynamics   the science of flight.

Aerofoil   a cross-section of the wing taken at right-angles to the span of the wing.

Aeromodelling   overall name for model-aircraft activities.

Aileron   movable control surfaces on the wings, which roll the plane to left or right.

Aileron differential   set-up in which the downward-moving aileron moves less distance than the upward-moving surface. Lowering the downward aileron too low creates induced drag and thus makes the wing skid rather than lift.

Airplane   US spelling of aeroplane.

AM (amplitude modulation)   simple system that modulates the actual radio wave.

Analogue   simple basic transmitted signal.

Anhedral   set-up in which the aeroplane wings are angled so that the tips are lower than the centre, used on high-wing aerobatic models. The Harrier Jet is a full-size version of such a set-up.

Antenna   alternative term for aerial.

Armature   central rotating core of an electric motor.

ARTF ('almost ready to fly')   describes the sort of kit that is now a very popular way of buying models.

Aspect ratio   ratio between the span and the width, or chord, of the wing.

BMFA (British Model Flying Association)   UK governing body for model-aircraft activities.

Ball link   pushrod connection with a link that 'snaps' on to a ball on the output arm.

Balsa wood   very light but very strong wood, once the only material used for model-aircraft construction. Still used extensively in model aeroplanes and modelling in general but has been superseded by modern composites in many areas of aeromodelling.

BARCS (British Association of Radio-Control Soarers)   all things gliders.

Battery   source of electrical power for radio.

BB (ball-bearing) engine   engine with ball race bearings on the crankshaft, which causes less friction than a plain metal-to-metal bearing and therefore gives longer life and more power.

BEC (battery elimination circuit)   electric motor speed controller that eliminates the need for a separate Rx battery by deriving radio power from the main power battery.

Belt drive   system used in some types of gearbox where a toothed belt is used to transfer the motor rpm from a small gear wheel to a larger gear wheel for lower ratio.

Biplane   aircraft with two main flying surfaces, or wings.

Brain fade   mental state in which a flyer suddenly forgets which way to move the controls. It can happens for no known reason, even to experienced and proficient people (*see* also 'Dumb thumb').

Brushes   spring-loaded carbon blocks that make continuous contact with the rotating core or commutator of an electric motor, while transferring the positive and negative voltage to the armature windings.

Brushless motors   vastly superior model electric motors using the three-phase system and no carbon brushes (which can cause radio interference).

Buddy box   system used in trainee pilot instruction to link pupil Tx and instructor Tx together by means of an umbilical cord. Loved by some instructors, but often claimed by others to give false confidence. Standard facility on most transmitters.

Bungee   method of launching sailplanes using stretched elastic to give launch effort.

CA (cyanoacrylate, or cyano)   instant glue available in various viscosities.

Canard   aircraft on which the tailplane is ahead of the main wing.

Carburettor   device that produces a combustible mixture by mixing fuel with air.

Case   outer cylindrical body of an electric motor.

Castor oil   viscous oil mixed with the fuel, giving lubrication of moving parts.

Centre of Gravity (CofG)   lateral balance point of an aircraft.

Clevis   device for connecting a control rod to a control horn on a control surface.

Closed loop   control surface operated by flexible wires under slight tension.

Cobalt type of brushed motor using special 'rare earth' magnets with stronger magnetic fields. Some brushless motors also use 'rare earth' magnets.

Cockpit part of the plane occupied by the pilot.

Commutator cylindrical arrangement of insulated metal bars connected to the coils of a dc electric motor.

Computer radio radio transmitter with electronically programmable set-up of control movements, which then stores each model set-up in a separate memory.

Connecting rod connects the piston to the crankshaft.

Control line model controlled by two long wires connected to a control handle.

Cowling part of the structure that encloses the engine.

Crankshaft shaft that converts the vertical movement of the piston into rotation.

Crystal device that controls the radiated radio frequency of the transmitter. The receiver also has its own matching crystal. All crystals carry a channel number.

Cylinder the unit where the fuel is compressed and ignited to produce the power stroke.

Cylinder head top of the cylinder, containing the glow plug or spark plug.

DEAC, button cells early generic name for Nicads.

'Dead stick' term used by a pilot to warn other flyers that his engine has stopped.

Delta set-up in which an aircraft has a triangular wing. Concorde is one example.

Diesel engine compression ignition engine that runs on a kerosene-based fuel with ether. Diesel engines were popular in Britain for a few years after the Second World War because the methanol that was required for glow-plug engines was not available. They were never popular in the USA, where methanol was always in plentiful supply.

Digital signal transmitted in binary code.

Dihedral set-up in which wingtips are higher than the centre of the wing, creating a shallow 'V' and giving pendulum stability. The actual degree of angle varies from design to design.

Direct drive set-up that uses an electric motor with the propeller fitted directly to the output shaft.

Down thrust downward tilt to the engine to counteract excessive wing lift.

Drag resistance to the forward motion of the model through the air.

Dual rates system that enables two different settings of a control surface movement.

Dumb thumb *see* 'Brain fade'.

Electric power use of rechargeable batteries to power electric motors.

Elevator movable control surface on the tailplane. Moves up or down to alter the angle of incidence (or of attack) of the wing. Also controls air speed.

Elevons   used on delta wings and flying wings, the ailerons also acting as elevators.

Epoxy glass   fibreglass coated with epoxy for a very strong covering.

Epoxy resin adhesive   two-part, resin hardener glue that is extremely strong, available in various types, from instant to 24-hour curing.

Fail-safe   system that cuts the engine and sets the flying controls to a predetermined setting if signal is lost. Mandatory on models over a certain weight.

Ferrite   standard iron magnets used in the cheaper ranges of brushed electric motors.

Fin   fixed vertical element of the tail-plane cluster.

Final approach   the landing part of the flight when lining up with the runway.

Firewall   main bulkhead in the fuselage to which the engine is attached.

Flaps   control surfaces on the wing, which increase the drag to lower the speed.

Flight box   container used to transport all the equipment used at the flying field, sometimes incorporating a model stand for starting and at-the-field maintenance.

Flux ring   iron ring clipped around a motor casing to improve the efficiency of the motor.

FM (frequency modulation)   signal in a modulated series of discharges.

Four-stroke   system in which the engine fires every other revolution.

Free flight   flying a model without any remote control system – still a popular hobby.

Frequency pennant   visual indication on the Tx of the frequency being used by flyer.

Frequency   waveband of the radio signal being transmitted to the aeroplane.

Fuel proofer   impervious coating for model-aircraft surfaces to ensure that raw fuel and oil do not seep into the internal structure and cause damage.

Fun flyer   model capable of performing seemingly impossible gyrations in the air. The manoeuvres are achieved by a very high power to weight ratio, and control surfaces often covering up to 45 per cent of the total flying surface area.

Fuselage   main body of aeroplane, acting as an anchor point for the flying surfaces and propulsion units.

Gearbox   gearing arrangement available in various ratios to drive larger propellers.

Geared   set-up that uses a gearbox on the output of the motor to allow propellers of a larger diameter to be turned.

Gimbal   ball-shaped mount for the transmitter control sticks, allowing movement in all directions.

Glitch   intermittent malfunctioning of RC system due to radio interference or metal-to-metal-generated electrical interference on the plane itself. Can be particularly bad where a metal-to-metal connection is used on the throttle connection.

GLOSSARY

Glow fuel   methanol mixed with lubricating oil and various ignition additives.

Glow plug   plug fitted with a platinum element that ignites methanol by catalytic action.

Glow-plug engine   engine that uses a platinum plug to ignite methanol fuel. Such engines are actually medium-compression diesel engines.

Gravity   the constant enemy of model flight, comes in the form of excess weight.

Ground effect   cushioning of the air against the ground as the aircraft comes in to land, which increases lift and prolongs the glide, sometimes past the end of the runway. It poses major problems for trainee model helicopter pilots, transferring from and to ground effect in the hover.

Ground loop   complete circle performed on the runway by the aircraft, often due to side winds. Tail draggers are more prone to it.

Gyro   controls the tail swing on a helicopter by adjusting the pitch of the tail rotor blades as it senses movement. Its introduction transformed model helicopter flying.

Hand launch   release of the plane from the hand.

'Hangar queen'   model that is built and all ready to fly but is never actually flown, usually due to extreme fear of the possible impending disaster.

Hangar rash   damage inflicted on the airframe during transit to and from the flying site.

Helicopter   flying machine with rotating wing (or blades).

High-wing   aircraft with the wings mounted on the top of the fuselage.

Incidence   angle of the wing relative to the fuselage centre or datum line.

Inline gearbox   gearbox that has the output shaft in line with the motor output shaft.

Inverted   flying the aeroplane upside down – or wrong way up.

Jet turbine   pure reaction engine in miniature operating as per full size.

Jetex   proprietary name for simple form of jet propulsion unit using dry pellets of fuel, as used in Second World War rocket-propelled shells. Popular in jet models of the 1950s.

Lithium polymer, lithium iron   high-density, high-energy cells, as used in mobile phones. Available for model use but best left to the expert due to their unstable nature.

LMA (Large Model Association)   governing body; 'large' means *large*.

Loop   basic aerobatic manoeuvre in the vertical plane.

Low-wing   aircraft with the wings mounted on the bottom of the fuselage.

Lubrication   application of light oil or grease to the bearings of a motor or gearbox.

Mid-air   colloquial name for an airborne collision between two models.

Mid-wing   model with the wing situated on the centre-line of the fuselage.

Mixer   mixes two or more of the basic controls to give improved control functions.

Modes   distribution of the basic four controls on the two transmitter sticks.

Monoplane   aircraft with one main flying surface, or wing.

Mounting   method of attaching the motor to the model.

Muffler   another word for exhaust silencer; *see* also 'Silencer'.

Neodym   another 'rare earth' type of magnetic material used in more powerful brushed motors.

Neutral stability   desirable set-up on aerobatic models giving accurate response to control inputs. Exactly opposite to trainers, which have built-in stability.

Nicad (nickel cadmium)   type of rechargeable battery used as the power source on transmitter and receiver. Also used in electric-powered model aeroplanes.

Nickel metal hydride (NiMH)   battery that is similar to a Nicad, but offers a longer duration of operation.

One-point landing   colloquial term for a dive – often terminal – into terra firma.

Outrunner   type of brushless motor where the outer casing is the rotating part of the motor and is fixed to the propeller, the central core remaining static.

Overdrive   application of voltage higher than the manufacturer's specified value to an electric motor.

Overshoot   situation in which an attempted landing has to be aborted due to various factors — for example, people on runway, plane on runway, approach too high — usually followed by a circuit and further landing attempt.

Ozone layer   slight sparking that occurs when the brushes rub against the commutator of the motor, producing very small amounts of ozone.

Parasol wing   wing mounted above the fuselage on struts.

Park flyer   very small, very light RC model, electric-powered, flown in small areas and indoors. Please note, insurance is still advisable.

Pattern plane   class of aerobatic plane designed to fly set aerial patterns.

PCM (pulse code modulation)   signal in binary code.

Peg board   physical system used to prevent two flyers operating on the same frequency.

Petrol   fuel used in spark ignition engines ('gas' in the USA).

Piston   unit that moves up and down in the cylinder and delivers the power stroke to the crankshaft, via the connecting rod.

Polyhedral   type of dihedral with more than one angle break in the wing.

Port wing   left wing, facing forward.

PPM (pulse position modulation)   position of each pulse representing the angular position of an analogue control on the transmitter.

Propeller balancer   device used to ensure that both prop blades have the same weight, to avoid damaging vibration. A vital tool.

Propeller   also known as the airscrew, unit that pulls the aircraft though the air.

Push rods   transmit movement from servos to control surfaces.

Pusher propeller   reverse pitch airscrew used where an engine is rear-mounted.

Quick link   spring-loaded detachable links used on pushrods. Another name for a clevis.

RC   radio-control.

ROG   rise off ground.

Radial engine   engine in which the cylinders are set around a central crankshaft.

Rate switch   switch that electronically reduces the throw of a control surface. Prevents over control in slow speed situations, landing, and so on.

Rating   optimum level of current a motor can handle safely.

Receiver   airborne link of the system that turns the radio signal into electrical pulses.

Re-kitting   colloquial term for the wreckage left after a terminal dive into terra firma.

Roll   basic aerobatic manoeuvre in the horizontal plane.

Rudder   movable control surface on the fin, mostly used to correct direction.

Running in   application of low voltage to a new motor to allow the carbon brushes to bed into the commutator without sparking or burning the contact surface.

Rx   shorthand for receiver.

SAA (Scottish Aeromodellers Association)   governing body in Scotland.

Sailplane   high-performance type of glider.

Scale model   accurate reproduction of full-size prototype.

Schnuerle porting   high-performance type of intake porting on a two-stroke engine.

Semi-scale   model giving the feel of a scale model but not accurate in every detail.

Servo   unit that turns the electrical pulse from the receiver into mechanical movement.

Shot down   term used when a plane crashes due to radio interference – sometimes outside source, but more often some other flyer switching-on, on your frequency.

Silencer   device designed to restrict the engine sound to an acceptable level.

Slope soarer   specialized glider that uses hillside slope lift to remain aloft.

Slow flyer   *see* 'Park flyer'.

Solo   a beginner's first totally unassisted flight with a controlled take-off and landing.

Spark ignition   system that uses an electrical spark to ignite the fuel, usually petrol.

Speed controller   feature that electronically controls the speed of an electric motor.

Speed   range of motors produced by Graupner. Robbe, Aeronaut and others market very similar motors under their own name.

Sport scale model   model designed to look like a scale model but with easy flying ability.

Sports model   model designed for general flying ability and good all-round use.

Stall   complete loss of lift, due to various aerodynamic factors.

Starboard wing   right wing, facing forward.

Stator   outer casing of a brushless motor carrying the windings.

Sticks   the two primary mechanical control functions on the transmitter.

STOL (short take-off and landing)   aircraft with special wings equipped with lift-enhancing flaps and slats.

Suppressors   small electronic components, also called 'capacitors', which are soldered between the motor + and – contacts to help reduce the radio interference produced by sparking between the carbon brushes and the rotating armature.

Synthetic oil   modern lubricating oil, which has replaced castor oil in most disciplines.

T tail   tailplane mounted on top of the fin.

Tail dragger   plane with single tail wheel and two main wheels.

Tailplane   fixed horizontal tail surface of an aeroplane.

Thermal   rising column of warm air capable of lifting gliders to a great height.

Thread lock   type of adhesive that locks up the thread of nuts and bolts in conditions where vibration is prevalent, for example, in helicopters.

Thrust   force produced by the motor/propeller combination, resulting in the forward movement of the model.

Timing   process of turning the back plate of a motor carrying the brushes in relation to the position of the magnets fixed to the case or 'can' to produce a 'hotter' motor.

Tip stall   loss of lift at one wingtip, when the wingtip that is stalling drops suddenly, this can turn the plane into a dive.

Torque   force produced within the motor that causes rotation.

Touch and go   landing and taking off again without stopping – a useful skill.

Trainer lead   trainer cord (*see* also 'Buddy box').

Trainer   model designed with in-built stability to give beginners thinking time.

Transmitter   the ground-based part of the radio system transmitting the control signal.

Trike   aircraft with a single nose wheel and two main wheels.

Tri-plane   aircraft with three main flying surfaces, or wings.

Tuned pipe   cone-shaped resonance pipe that augments the engine power. Used on two-stroke motorbikes, and originally developed for the V1 flying bomb.

Two-stroke   system in which the engine fires on every revolution.

Tx   shorthand for transmitter.

Tyro   posh term for beginner.

UHF (ultra-high frequency)   excellent, interference-free waveband, now nearly defunct, owing to very high unit cost.

Under-camber   concave curve on the underside of some aerofoils. Little used in RC applications due to very narrow speed range. Still popular in free-flight models.

Undercarriage   arrangement of wheels to support the aircraft on the ground.

V tail   format in which the tailplane and fin are combined into a single V structure.

Vortices   drag-inducing rotating currents of air at the wingtip caused by the pressure differential of the air flowing over the top and lower surfaces of the wing.

Warp   unwanted twist in an intended flat wing surface. At best, it can lead to some very interesting variations in the flight pattern; at worst, it can spell disaster.

Wash-out   set-up in which the angle of attack of the wing at the tips is less than at the wing centre. This helps prevent tip stalling and subsequent loss of control.

Winch   used to launch model sailplanes to a great height. Usually electric-powered.

Windings   the lacquered copper wires that are wound around the formers of an electric motor, producing a magnetic field when a current is passed through them.

Wing chord   distance from the leading edge to the trailing edge.

Wing loading   ratio of the aircraft weight to the area of the wing lifting surface.

Wing   main supporting surface of the aircraft. Can take many forms.

Z-bend   Z-shaped bend in the wire end of a pushrod, used to attach the pushrod to a servo output arm.

Z-bend pliers   special pliers used to form the Z-bend in piano wire.

USEFUL WEBSITES

From time to time you may need to contact organizations and other information providers associated with the radio-control flying scene in your home territory. The following is a list of some of those official organizations, along with their websites, which may prove useful to you.

International: FAI, or Fédération Aéronautique Internationale (www.fai.org)

UK: BMFA, or British Model Flying Association (www.bmfa.org)

USA: AMA, or Academy of Model Aeronautics (www.modelaircraft.org)

Argentina: FAA, or Federaçion Argentinia de Modelismo (www.faa.org.ar)

Australia: Model Aeronautical Association of Australia (www.maaa.asn.au)

Austria: Austrian RC Model Association (www.lexsoft.at/aeroclub)

Brazil: Confederação Brasileira de Aeromodelismo (www.cobra.org.br)

Canada: MAAC, or Model Aeronautics Association of Canada (www.maac.ca)

Denmark: RC-Unionen Denmark (www.rc-unionen.dk)

France: Fédération Française d'Aéromodelisme (www.ffam.asso.fr)

Germany: Deutscher Modellflieger Verband (www.dmfv.de)

Italy: FIAM (www.fiamaero.it)

Netherlands: Federatie Modelvliegers Spaarnwoude (www.airtoi.com/fmse.htm); KNVvL Modelvliegsport (www.modelvliegsport.nl)

New Zealand: New Zealand Model Aeronautical Association (www.nzmaa.org.nz)

Portugal: Federação Portuguesa de Aeromodelismo (www.fpam.pt)

Scotland: Scottish Aeromodellers Association (www.saaweb.org.uk)

South Africa: South African Model Aircraft Association (www.icon.co.za/~samaa/)

Sweden: Sveriges Modellflygförbund (www.modellflygforbund.se)

Switzerland: Swiss Aeromodelling Association (www.modellflug.ch)

Turkey: Turkish Aeronautical Association (www.thk.org.tr/yeni/indexeng.htm)

INDEX